THE ECONOMICS OF CENTRAL BANKING

This book offers a comprehensive analysis of central banks, and aims to demystify them for the general public, which is the only way to have a rational debate about them and ultimately to make them truly accountable.

The book originates from the author's graduate lectures on Central Banking at the University of Frankfurt J.W. Goethe. It contains an overview of all the key questions surrounding central banks and their role in the economy. It leads the reader from the more established concepts (including monetary theory and historical experience), necessary to have a good grasp of modern central banking, to the more open and problematic questions, which are being debated within academic and financial market circles. This structure enables readers without specific knowledge of central banks or monetary economics to understand the current challenges.

The book has three defining characteristics, which set it apart from competing titles: first, it is pitched at the general public and uses simple and entertaining language. Second, it is rooted in, and makes frequent reference to, recent academic research, based on content for a graduate level course. Third, the author thinks 'out of the box' in order to describe the possible evolution of central banks (including the prospect of their disappearance), and not only the status quo.

Livio Stracca is the Head of International Policy Analysis at the European Central Bank and Adjunct Professor at the University of Frankfurt J.W. Goethe, Germany. The views expressed belong to the author and are not necessarily shared by the European Central Bank.

THE ECONOMICS OF CENTRAL BANKING

Livio Stracca

LONDON AND NEW YORK

First published 2018
by Routledge
2 Park Square, Milton Park, Abingdon, Oxon OX14 4RN

and by Routledge
711 Third Avenue, New York, NY 10017

Routledge is an imprint of the Taylor & Francis Group, an informa business

© 2018 Livio Stracca

The right of Livio Stracca to be identified as author of this work has been asserted by them in accordance with sections 77 and 78 of the Copyright, Designs and Patents Act 1988.

All rights reserved. No part of this book may be reprinted or reproduced or utilised in any form or by any electronic, mechanical, or other means, now known or hereafter invented, including photocopying and recording, or in any information storage or retrieval system, without permission in writing from the publishers.

Trademark notice: Product or corporate names may be trademarks or registered trademarks, and are used only for identification and explanation without intent to infringe.

British Library Cataloguing in Publication Data
A catalogue record for this book is available from the British Library

Library of Congress Cataloging in Publication Data
A catalog record for this book has been requested

ISBN: 978-1-138-29709-8 (hbk)
ISBN: 978-1-138-49671-2 (pbk)
ISBN: 978-1-315-09952-1 (ebk)

Typeset in Bembo
by Taylor & Francis Books

CONTENTS

List of illustrations		*vi*
Foreword		*vii*
1	Money and central banks	1
2	How monetary policy works: the mainstream model	18
3	Three questions on the mainstream model	35
4	The zero lower bound problem	48
5	Financial stability and the lender of last resort function of central banks	71
6	Will paper currency disappear and will this be a problem?	92
7	Will we ever have a global central bank?	102
8	Will central banks disappear?	119
Index		*130*

ILLUSTRATIONS

Figures

4.1 Short-term interest rates in the world's major industrialised economies. The Wu-Xia 'shadow' federal funds rate is an indicator of the interest rate that takes into account the effect of non-standard measures such as QE.   54

4.2 Size of the central bank balance sheet in main industrialised countries, rescaled at August 2007 = 100.   62

4.3 The remarkable stability of annual CPI inflation in OECD countries.   67

6.1 Currency in circulation as a share of Gross Domestic Product in the world's four largest economies.   96

7.1 There is much more variability in the exchange rate than in relative consumer prices in the world's two largest economies, the US and the euro area. Levels are set at 1999 = 100.   111

8.1 CPI inflation in the United States, 1800 to present.   127

Table

1.1 Stylised central bank balance sheets   11

FOREWORD

Many colleagues, students, family and friends helped me to shape and finalise this book. First and foremost, I would like to thank countless students of mine at the University of Frankfurt J.-W. Goethe. After all, the book is based on the lectures I gave at the Central Banking course in that university, and it benefits from the many intelligent questions I received from students, coming from all corners of the world.

I would also very much like to thank Laurence Ball, Lorenzo Bini Smaghi, John Cochrane, Alex Cukierman, Benjamin Friedman, Charles Goodhart, Gabriel Glöckler, Ed Nelson, Nobuhiro Kiyotaki, Ken Rogoff, Stephanie Schmitt-Grohe, Narayana Kocherlakota, Eswar Prasad, Ricardo Reis, Valerie Saintot, Cedric Tille and many ECB colleagues for either commenting on the draft or giving me useful suggestions on the topics covered in the book.

My wife, Simonetta, and my father read parts of the book and gave very useful suggestions, in particular with an eye to making it clearer for a general readership.

Kristina Abbotts and Laura Hussey at Routledge have been very helpful and patient in dealing with my questions. This is my first book and their support has been particularly important. I would also like to warmly thank two anonymous reviewers for Routledge, who materially improve the scope and structure of the book.

Finally, it is important to explicitly mention that, although my long experience in the European Central Bank has certainly helped to share my views on central banks, everything in the book should be seen as my personal opinion and is not necessarily shared by the institution to which I am affiliated. Likewise, any remaining errors are only my own.

1
MONEY AND CENTRAL BANKS

Central bankers are increasingly in the limelight of public attention, monitored with the same obsession traditionally reserved to celebrities. In the post crisis environment they have greatly enlarged their span of action, resulting in what some observers regard as over-reach and mission creep. Central bankers also venture more and more into new fields, speaking on a large range of issues that were traditionally well outside their remit, including, for example, climate change or the quality of schools. One century ago there were only 15 central banks in the world; there are now over 200.

Increased public attention and scrutiny is to be welcomed. Central banks are and always have been important. They do matter for citizens' welfare, and should be held accountable for their actions, which they typically pride themselves to be. At the same time, increased public attention has not been accompanied by a rise in public trust in them. Quite the opposite in fact – trust in central banks is on the decline worldwide in the wake of the global financial crisis. This is visible not only in angry blogs ruminating on worldwide conspiracy theories of world domination by bankers and their associates but also, and more relevantly, in survey data. It is a worrying trend, because central bankers as unelected officials ultimately derive their legitimacy from public trust. They cannot perform well for long without it.

Falling trust is also accompanied by enduring lack of knowledge about central banks and their actions. Money and finance are often seen as ephemeral concepts, created out of thin air, now as ever. To be fair, we don't know much about what the public knows. My own, surely very casual and anecdotal, evidence suggests that the knowledge gap is worryingly large. For example, it is quite remarkable that very few people appear to realise that nominal interest rates are bound at zero – not an irrelevant curiosity but a fact that alone may well explain why millions of jobs have been lost, as we will see in Chapter 4.

In one of the few available studies, Dutch researchers investigated public knowledge about the European Central Bank (ECB).[1] Respondents to the Dutch survey appear to know relatively little about the ECB. Moreover, knowledge appears to be positively correlated with social status and desire to be informed about it. Interestingly, though not surprisingly, information on central banks is mainly derived from media. And it matters: more knowledge about the ECB is associated with a better ability to formulate correct inflation expectations, important for household decision-making. Another study on UK citizens reaches similar conclusions.[2]

Knowledge matters both in order to buttress trust in central banks – there is indeed evidence of a positive correlation between the two – but also for central bank accountability. As long as the public is not informed or does not understand what central banks do, their representatives in parliaments are equally unlikely to exercise their prerogatives to hold the central bank to account in an effective way. There is no true accountability without knowledge.

The main aim of this book is to strengthen the general knowledge and understanding of what central banks are and do. Clearly, one of the reasons why knowledge is poor is that people have better things to do in their life than poring over central bank balance sheets. Still, I will try to show that key questions around central banking are both accessible to non-economists and intellectually interesting, in some cases even entertaining. The challenge I want to pose to myself in this book is to explain modern central banking, in its open and problematic aspects, to a wider audience. Hopefully this has led me to a better understanding of some issues – there is nothing as instructive as having to explain to a non-technical audience for recognising our own ignorance, often glossed over without a real and deep understanding under the cover of technical jargon.

Therefore, this book goes over all main questions surrounding modern central banking, starting from the very question of why money exists. Although the way in which the material and the ideas are presented is hopefully original, in fact I do not claim to be breaking new ground in almost anything the book covers. For ease of exposition, sources are contained in the notes at the end of each chapter and not reported along the way, but it should be clear that the book is based on a large body of policy and research work, overwhelmingly produced by others. My contribution has mainly been to summarise and present this large body of work in an accessible and hopefully entertaining way. Another contribution of this book is to provide an 'update' to earlier books on central banks, which is important since a lot has happened in central banking in the past two decades.[3]

Any analysis of central banks must necessarily begin with the question of money's existence. After all, what central banks contribute to society is essentially money, or monetary services.

Let us then get started with that question. Why do we need money at all?

The inefficiency of barter

In modern financial systems money is a slippery and elusive entity. However, the origins of money are very material indeed, and indeed the name of most currencies used today can be traced back to measures of weight – this is obvious in some cases, for example for the pound or the peso.

A good place to start to make progress in understanding monetary economics is to note that in a complex and specialised economy barter is a very inefficient form of trade. The absence of a double coincidence of wants (I produce bananas, you produce pears, but I want apples) is often mentioned as the key reason why barter is inefficient, but it is only one of them. If transactions were completely costless, double coincidence of wants would not be a problem by itself. I can sell my bananas to you, and with your pears in my hand, I can exchange them for apples with somebody else. In fact, this is what would happen in all standard general equilibrium models in economics that are currently taught at graduate schools – these models are practically 'money-less' and money is at best appended in an ad hoc way. More generally, the transaction could involve the exchange between a specific good and any good that can serve as a numeraire, say apples. The numeraire could then be used in exchange for any other good, after taking into account factors like expected depreciation - the apple may rot and lose value before the next transaction. For example, an apple as a numeraire can be exchanged for 2 pears and 1.5 bananas, which completely defines the price system in this three-good economy.

The price level in this economy without transaction costs is simply the *relative* price of the numeraire with respect to a representative basket of goods and services. Any good can be used in this way, in principle, as long as it has some intrinsic value. It is important to keep in mind therefore that money would not need to exist in the absence of transaction costs, even in the absence of a double coincidence of wants.

But transaction costs do exist, as purchasing and selling do require time and effort. The economics of transaction costs is not an easy one to develop, as it is difficult to conceive general rules. Transaction costs are probably very transaction-specific and contingent on the space and time where the transaction takes place. For this reason, it is hard to build a general theory of transaction costs and this is one of the main difficulties eventually confronting monetary theory.

Key functions of money

According to the typical textbook description, money has three main functions: store of value, unit of account, and means of exchange. The first function is arguably the least important and is more a precondition for the other two: if something is not seen as a store of value at least to some extent, it is unlikely to be used in transactions. The two other functions are crucial but also, importantly, closely intertwined. In particular, the use of something as means of payment – implying a role in minimising transaction costs – makes it easier for the same entity to also be the unit of account. There is a reason, for example, why prices are expressed is euros in Europe and not, say, in US dollars. The US dollar is an excellent unit of account, but the fact is that in Europe euro banknotes are used for transactions.

There is also the other direction of causality: something used as a unit of account is more likely to be used also as a means of payment – although, in my opinion, the causality running from the means of payment function to the unit of account function is the stronger one.

Commodity monies

If a good is used as an intermediate step in trade, it plays a monetary function which may add to its intrinsic value as a commodity. This is the case of commodity money; indeed as just discussed all goods can in principle become commodity monies if transaction costs are zero. Suppose that bananas, pears and apples all provide the same utility and are equally difficult to produce. If for some reason pears are more amenable to transact on, then pears may acquire a monetary value in addition to their intrinsic value.

In practice, not all goods serve this purpose equally well. A good that is subject to large fluctuations in value (say, hit by frequent demand and supply shocks, or with rapid depreciation) may not have a monetary function and may even increase transaction costs. Even more damaging for the transaction role of any commodity is asymmetric information on the value between the buyer and the seller. (In economics, asymmetric information denotes a situation where one party of a contract has more information than the other and can use it to his advantage.) For this reason, say, used cars are not a good form of money. Commodity-based monetary standards, such as gold and silver, have been based on goods that are relatively scarce and difficult to produce, and also – perhaps more importantly – relatively easy to verify.

An ideal form of commodity money should be relatively scarce, but also not too scarce. Diamonds, for example, have never had any monetary value. For the opposite reason, water can hardly ever be used as money (except, perhaps, in the middle of a desert). The commodity must also be divisible, of course, so as to be used in all transactions – another characteristic where diamonds would fail since even the tiniest of them would be too valuable to pay for a small transaction. Portability is another obvious characteristic of good money – hence immobile assets can hardly acquire a monetary value unless portable rights can be written on them.

Fiat money

If we dissociate the monetary value from the intrinsic value, we can create fiat money – a good *only* used as an intermediate element in order to transact in other goods – that is intrinsically worthless. The term 'fiat money' derives from Latin, where 'fiat' means 'let it be'.

How can something without intrinsic value (with a relative price of zero against any other commodity) arise as a credible means of payment? It can only do as a result of a social convention based on collective imagination. A society can *pretend* that something intrinsically worthless has positive worth if used as an intermediate element in transactions. A euro coin is, objectively speaking, almost worthless – not completely worthless in fact because it is costly to mint, but almost. I can produce a banana, exchange it for a euro coin and buy one apple with the euro coin. This means that the relative price of a (worthless) euro coin vs. a banana is 1. It is easy to generalise the concept to an entire basket of goods.

The economic system faces a fundamental coordination problem with fiat money. In theory, any form of paper currency and any other worthless object could have a monetary role. Evidently there are economies of scale in having only one, or at most a few, monies, in the same way as it is more efficient to speak one language rather than several languages. The government can play a useful role in coordinating expectations on a particular means of payment; this is a view traditionally emphasised by Cartalists, who point out that sovereign power and money creation are closely associated, and even commodity monies could not exist or circulate without some government intervention. Government-issued banknotes, officially defined as legal tender, represent a way to reach that coordination. We will come back to the role of the government in money creation in the last chapter of the book.

An ideal solution to the inefficiency of barter: a ledger of transactions

Imagine an economy populated by persons who produce different goods, for example each person can pick only one kind of fruit from fruit trees. At the same time, each consumer wants a composite good (say, a mix of fruits); all consumers are perfectly honest and truthful, a characteristic whose importance will be clear in a moment. People buy different goods from other people but need to find somebody else who wants their good, and this takes shopping time that is costly and wasteful. This explains the inefficiency of barter. It is quite easy to see that a benevolent social planner, who cares about the performance of the whole economy, would want shopping time to be reduced, and an ideal solution would be to establish a ledger of transactions. Whenever a person sells the good that he produces he receives a positive entry in a register for the amount that he sold defined in terms of the composite good. When he purchases another good for his consumption, his entry in the register is reduced accordingly. This arrangement allows each person to buy and sell without the need to find a counterpart who wants the good he produces.

But now suppose that people are not honest and would walk away from their obligations, especially if they exceed their dues, in the ledger. Therefore, the ideal solution of the register is not feasible because there would be too much cheating and distrust. A good second best solution is for something, that we call money, to 'proxy' for the entry in the register that is readily accepted for payment. That something can be intrinsically valuable, such as gold, but also not so, such as a contract like paper currency; the idea that money is a substitute for the ledger of all transactions is more evident for monies that are not intrinsically valuable, but rather give the right to purchase a basket of goods and services, now or in the future. In a sense, money is the first example of a financial asset.[4]

Evil is the root of all money

Money, especially intrinsically worthless money, can be seen as a second best alternative to a credit-based system based on a ledger of past transactions. Rather than marking a debit or credit into the ledger, the transfer of a unit of money symbolises the same action and makes the registration unnecessary. Both fiat money and a registration system are entirely the result of imagination and social convention – though the effect of that imagination is very tangible in the form of transactions that would otherwise not take place.

Part of the problem with a ledger is that credit history is unobservable, so preventing cheating would not be feasible – or at least it was not feasible in the past due to limitations in credit register technology. In the words of Nobuhiro Kiyotaki (Princeton University) and John Moore (University of Edinburgh), 'evil is the root of all money'.[5]

To recap, money is essentially a good second-best and low-tech recordkeeping system, which tracks who contributed or did not contribute to trade. One item used as money is like a symbol saying 'I have contributed and, in an ideal register of credits and debits, I would have a plus'. As pointed out very aptly by Narayana Kocherlakota at the University of Rochester, 'money is memory'.[6]

We will see later in Chapter 8 that technological advances might make the first best solution, a ledger of all past transactions, feasible but also that technology is not all that matters, public trust and the quality of institutions may be even more important.

Characteristics of good money

In monetary economics it is often emphasised that good money should be elastic, but not too elastic. By 'elastic' we mean a characteristic of its supply in relation to the amount or type of transactions for which it is used. A very elastic supply allows the economy to increase the quantity of money very rapidly and easily if there is a demand for it.

The fact that money should be 'elastic, but not too elastic' is admittedly not an exceedingly precise characterisation, but it captures the important notion that there is an optimal middle way between scarcity and abundance that makes something a potential candidate for providing monetary services. In particular, the cost of production should be positive but small. What is optimal in real life is, of course, an entirely empirical question.

In addition, an ideal form of money should be divisible, portable, and verifiable. Note that nothing here suggests that money should necessarily be intrinsically valuable, though some forms of money are; because it is a proof of past contribution, it is fundamentally a social contrivance. Charles Kindleberger (the late author of *Manias, Panics, and Crashes*) noted that money is a bit like language, a common good derived from social convention.[7]

Another slightly more sophisticated desirable characteristic of money is that it should be *information insensitive*.[8] Being information insensitive essentially means that no party should have better information about the value of the good or asset that is used as money. In other words, the value of money should not be 'revealed' by the release of information because everybody should have the necessary information to value it in the first place. For example, the stock of a firm is unlikely to be used as money, because it would be sensitive to the release of information about the firm and its managers would have an information advantage over its valuation compared with outsiders.

Valuation of money in relation to its quantity

In any monetary system, the price level can be defined as the inverse of the value of the monetary standard against a basket of goods and services. For example, if the monetary standard is an ounce of silver, the price level is defined as the inverse of what that ounce of silver can buy. Therefore, the price level is ultimately a question of asset valuation, if money can be considered to be a real asset (commodity money) or a financial asset (fiat money).

The next question is whether the quantity of money has an impact on its value. There may be a close relationship in many situations, but it is less direct than one could think at first sight. In the case of an intrinsically valuable commodity, the quantity of the commodity will influence the value of that commodity vs. other goods, and normally a demand curve is downward sloped, implying that there is *negative* relationship between the quantity of the commodity and its price. For example, a surprise increase in the supply of gold tends to reduce its price, and hence *increase* the price level defined in terms of gold.

For intrinsically worthless money, however, the relationship is more tenuous. If fiat money is a financial asset, we know that the quantity in circulation of a financial asset plays little role, if any at all, in the expected return on that asset. For example, a financial asset promising to be valued exactly as an apple all the time will trade at par with an apple, irrespective of how many such assets circulate in the economy.

For a financial asset commonly used as means of payment, however, the quantity may matter to some extent because it is easier to make payments if the asset is more abundant. For example, suppose that in the fruit tree economy there is only one single piece of paper that can be used as money. One can imagine that there would be a queue of people waiting to use that single piece of paper to carry out their transaction, and that this would slow down trade but also increase the monetary value of the piece of paper. This would in turn lead to a fall in the price level defined in that piece of paper due to its scarcity.

The following example helps to clarify matters. Suppose you receive a document entitling you to go on holiday on a cruise ship. Although the document is worthless in principle in the strictly physical terms of the paper it is written on, it still has an economic value because it gives the right to obtain the holiday. It derives its value from the legal system which forces the issuer to deliver on the promise to provide a paid holiday – it is as 'worthless' as any contract or obligation that is supported by law – that is, not at all worthless. Now suppose that you do not like cruise ships and you prefer to give the document to your friend John, in exchange for a motorbike that he has; John then redeems the holiday and extinguishes the right given by the document. The same document will support two transactions at the same price. But you can also think of a twist: it may take time for John to give you the motorbike, and John would have preferred to take the holiday earlier if he had the document in his hand, so eventually the two transactions do not take place, and the document is now worth as much as the paper it is printed on.

This serves to illustrate the broader point that an equilibrium with the same price level may be supported by different levels of the 'money supply', as long as money can circulate at different velocities – where velocity is defined as the speed at which the entity called money changes hands. If velocity is infinitely flexible (which is unlikely, because otherwise why would it help reducing transaction costs in the first place?), then there is no link at all between the quantity of money and prices.

Inside and outside money

Once a particular good has been identified as money, it is possible to construct an entire edifice of bilateral or multilateral obligations based on it. The overall size of the (imaginary) edifice can be a large multiple of the original set. I can, for example, agree to receive 10 silver coins today and promise to give back 11 of them next year. More complicated contracts can also be built, of course. For example, I could borrow 10 coins and promise to pay back 20 coins if my investment project succeeds and 5 otherwise.

A useful distinction is therefore made between 'outside money', i.e. the good that is originally used as money, and 'inside money', the private contracts that are built around outside money and are convertible into it. For example, bank deposits are inside money and are convertible into outside money, namely banknotes and coins. The names 'outside' and 'inside' refer to whether the monetary asset is generated inside the private sector economy or outside it.

The key difference between inside and outside money is that only the latter is *irredeemable*, namely convertible into nothing else than goods and services. One euro, or one dollar, can only be converted into one euro, or one dollar. By contrast, inside money derives its value by its being convertible into outside money.

Hierarchies of money

Perhaps one of the first forms of inside money, common during the Middle Ages, was based on strongboxes used to store metal coins. Rich merchants found it inconvenient to carry along large quantities of heavy (and easy to steal) metal coins, and preferred to safely deposit them with moneychangers, the forerunners of modern banks. Although we obviously do not use strongboxes anymore, bank deposits are ultimately just the same, namely a promise by the banker to pay a certain amount of a *physical* asset, banknotes. A certificate given by a moneychanger in the Middle

Ages can qualify as money only if the holder can be absolutely sure about its validity and authenticity.

Here we can see the concept of information insensitivity in action: suppose that I, merchant of the Middle Ages and holder of a certificate giving me the right to withdraw 100 silver coins, offer you this certificate as a payment for a certain good or service. If I have private information about the honesty of the moneychanger, you may rightly suspect that I am using this information to my advantage. For example, I could have certificates from two moneychangers, one honest and one less honest. It is in my interest, not yours, to give you the certificate from the less honest moneychanger, and by anticipating this you may want to ask for a discount on the face value of the payment. For example, rather than accepting the certificate as payment for 100 silver coins, you will do so for 50 silver coins.

More generally, there may be *imperfect substitutability* between different forms of (inside and outside) money. Here it is useful to introduce the concept of *hierarchies of money*. Any 'money' can be created at will by the private sector, but is always at the risk of expropriation depending on the bargaining power of the parties. You and I can agree with a third person that you owe me 1000 silver coins, I owe the third person 1000 silver coins, and the third person owes you 1000 silver coins. Strictly speaking, we have increased the supply of inside money out of thin air, without any change in net positions and without any exchange of good or services. But the system of interlocking liabilities that we created is very fragile because it is vulnerable to cheating by any of the three parties, and we are not sure that a third party should accept any of our newly created promises to pay as a payment, or do so without a heavy discount. The inside money created out of thin air is therefore a poor substitute for the real thing, and comes far lower in the hierarchy of monies.

Interesting recent work by Perry Mehrling at Barnard College describes an economy where the hierarchy between different forms of money flattens and steepens, depending on economic circumstances.[9] Because many forms of inside money depend on trust (that third parties will respect their obligations), fluctuations in trust will also determine the hierarchy of money, both over time and in different locations. For example, in countries with low trust some forms of inside money will be far lower in the hierarchy and be heavily discounted vis-à-vis outside money. Central banks sit at the top of the money hierarchy and they exploit their unique position to influence the economy, as we will see in action along various dimensions in the book.

The demise of commodity money and the rise of fiat money and central banks

Arguably the most important monetary innovation of the past century has been the demise of commodity money, and notably of the Gold Standard (a system where gold is the monetary standard) that is its most prominent incarnation, in favour of fiat money issued by central banks.

It is useful to recall that for most of history, including modern history, there was no central bank and especially no central bank in the modern sense of the term. We now understand a central bank as a bank whose liabilities are the final means of payment, but this was not necessarily true during, for example, the Gold Standard. The world has survived without central banks for a very long time. Canada, for example, only established a central bank in 1935, and yet was and is a very successful economy.

Although the Sveriges Riksbank was actually founded slightly earlier, the birth of central banks can be dated at 1694 with the establishment of the Bank of England. It was a very different entity from the Bank of England we know today; it was a profit-oriented private company, certainly with no intention to run monetary policy for the benefit of the country. The history of central banking in the United States is even more recent and more troubled; a federal central bank, the Federal Reserve of the United States, was not established until 1913, and largely thanks to a bank panic that happened a few years earlier in 1907.

Central banks are now part and parcel of a system based on fiat money, but for most of their existence they have been tied to a metallic standard (namely a standard build on something made of some metal), based on gold or silver (or both). Gold was often considered the most stable commodity standard, and some indeed still think so. The golden era of the Gold Standard was the period from around 1870 to the early 1930s, led by Britain.[10] Gold coins (often called 'specie') existed much earlier, even in the Roman Empire. In Florence during the Renaissance, for example, florins were made out of gold.

Gold is in rather short supply; according to some estimates, the whole stock of gold available in the world and already extracted from the ground could fit into a cube of just 20 meters each side, though this is not uncontroversial and there are different estimates. While there is a lot of gold still in the ground, it is costly and risky to extract, and gold mines have a notorious reputation the world over for dangerous conditions and high risk of injury and death. Gold, like other precious metals, can also be divisive for societies. In African countries such as Congo, for example, gold is a source of income for armed groups that foment instability, the so-called 'conflict gold'.

Be it as it may, gold is typically the preferred choice if the objective is to limit the supply of outside money and to keep prices stable or falling. It symbolises 'good money' in the mind of those actors of society who have an interest in keeping prices stable or falling (often creditors), but the enemy of those who may gain from inflation or fear deflation (often debtors), who tend to prefer silver that is in more abundant supply. Monetary issues of this type sometimes intrude in the political debate. Famously, William Jennings Bryan, at the United States Democratic National Convention in Chicago in 1896, vowed "You shall not crucify mankind upon a cross of gold". It was even argued that the book and later celebrated movie *The Wizard of Oz* is an allegory of the debate on the gold or silver standard in the US in the late 19th century.[11]

TABLE 1.1 Stylised central bank balance sheets

Gold Standard		Fiat money	
Assets	*Liabilities*	*Assets*	*Liabilities*
Gold	Banknotes (redeemable into gold)	Whatever, including some gold (composition largely irrelevant)	Banknotes (irredeemable)

Because gold is impractical as a means of payment in everyday life, under the Gold Standard central banks (but often also commercial banks) had the right to issue banknotes backed by, and convertible into, gold. The balance sheet of that central bank during the Gold Standard therefore had gold on the asset side, and banknotes on the liabilities side. In a fiat money system like the one prevailing today in most countries, this is not the case anymore. The liabilities of the central bank are simply the ultimate means of payment by law; what the central bank has on the asset side is quite irrelevant for the functioning of the monetary system, and, at least as a first approximation, has no bearing on the properties of its liabilities as money. Table 1.1 reports a stylised representation of central bank balance sheets in the Gold Standard and in the current fiat money system.

It is worth adding here that even under the Gold Standard, unless it is a pure bullion standard where gold coins circulate as a means of payment, price stability is not guaranteed. For that to happen there needs to be full trust that the convertibility between the medium of exchange and gold will be ensured, now and in the future. And in history convertibility has been far from guaranteed, over and over again.

According to the 'real bills doctrine', popular especially among private bankers in the 19th century, the institution issuing money always needs to back up fiat money with reserves denominated in something 'real'; only in this way will money creation not be inflationary. In the Gold Standard, for example, central bank liabilities were backed by gold. Proponents of the real bills doctrine would argue, for example, that in a fiat money system the central bank, in order to ensure convertibility with real goods and services, should have, on its assets side, a basket of goods and services, or at least something giving it a right to purchase that basket. In the absence of the 'real' assets in the assets side of the balance sheet there will be nothing to back up the liabilities side and to anchor its valuation to something real. Although the theory itself is now widely forgotten, there are traces of it in modern monetary policy making, as we will soon see.

The fall of the Gold Standard

The Gold Standard was the immediate predecessor of the system of fiat money in which we live nowadays. As mentioned, its best period was between 1870 and 1914, when it underpinned an expansion of economic activity and a high degree of openness to trade, what we now call globalisation.[12] It was a regime with London at its apex as the world's financial centre, and the pound sterling as the main international currency. This period (and the Gold Standard with it) is often looked back on as a period of unrivalled optimism and prosperity. At the same time, this order (and the Gold Standard with it) came crashing down at the onset of World War I. Indeed, a less well known consequence of the start of World War I was the collapse of the Gold Standard, triggered by runs on most currencies including the dominant currency at the time, the pound sterling. With gold reserves depleted and governments under pressure to finance war expenditure, convertibility was suspended and only resumed, in a half-hearted and controversial way, in the post-war period.

The inter-war period saw several attempts to resurrect the Gold Standard in the major powers, but none of them proved durable and in particular did not withstand the deflationary shock of the Great Depression. Ultimately in the early 1930s the Gold Standard was abandoned and a period of monetary disorder, characterised by inconvertibility both between currencies and with gold, followed – a period also punctuated by protectionism and fall in international trade, not to speak of course of armed conflict between the major powers. The Bretton Woods conference in 1944 attempted to restore the old order in a new way, where the US dollar largely took the role previously taken by gold. However, this order also proved to be temporary, and it collapsed little more than 25 years later.

Why did the Gold Standard collapse?

The demise of the Gold Standard was clearly not the result of an optimal design by policy-makers to provide the world with better money, but rather the victim of dramatic political events and in particular World War I. However, there are some underlying economic reasons why the Gold Standard was sub-optimal and fragile. There are essentially three problems with the Gold Standard, two of which related to the practical complications of using metal coins (although these problems were largely overcome by the turn of the 20th century) and the last one the most important to understand the collapse of the system in the first half of the 20th century.

A first, more mundane reason is that metal coins are not a very efficient means of payment in a modern economy. Debasing metal coins was easy, although it used to attract harsh punishments.[13] It may be more difficult to debase gold coins than other metals, which was one possible reason for the success of gold, though this view is refuted in some contributions. Therefore, a pure specie standard is very unlikely to be practical in a modern economy.

Second and related, the *big problem of small change* looms large. Here we should recall that governments, notably in Europe, often fixed an official price for coins. When the price of coins was low (namely the general price level was high) it was convenient to melt coins as their metal value was higher than the monetary value. As a consequence, coins of different metals and denomination periodically disappeared and re-appeared, which was the so-called 'coinage problem'. It was actually the 'good money' that tends to be hoarded and hence disappears from circulation first, a phenomenon known as the *Gresham Law*. (The law takes its name from Sir Thomas Gresham, a British banker and merchant of the 16th century, but it appears that he never actually meant this to be a general law and it was only attributed to him posthumously.)

As noted by Tom Sargent (New York University) and Francois Velde (Federal Reserve of Chicago) in a well-known book, small denomination coins are clearly more efficient in trade (especially retail trade), so to ensure that in equilibrium the public holds both high and low denomination coins they often traded at a discount (namely at a price lower than their face value), or had lower metal content, sometimes dramatically so. Hence small coins eventually become more valuable as metal than as coins, meaning that they are melted and disappear from circulation, compounding the problem.[14]

Third and more fundamentally, however, a commodity based monetary system is inherently inflexible. Sooner or later, the price level is hostage to the constraints and vagaries of the market of the particular commodity used as money. This is the main reason why the Gold Standard proved to be eventually unsustainable; it was vulnerable to political (two world wars) and economic (Great Depression) shocks – although it is also a legitimate question to ask what other monetary system would have survived shocks of that size.

Fiat money, by contrast, has all of the flexibility that commodity money lacks – even too much of it. In particular, the most important downside of fiat money is that it is too cheap to produce, which may encourage the issuer to produce too much of it, creating inflation. However, the link between money supply and inflation is not as automatic as is often argued. To understand this, we need to address the quantity theory of money, and move closer to monetary policy and to central banks.

The quantity theory of money is an empirical question, not a general law

Obviously in a non-monetary system – not only barter but also a credit-based system – there is no such concept as the price level in the way we normally intend it in a monetary economy. The price level is nothing else than the value of money defined in terms of a certain basket of goods, which may include all goods produced by society but also a subset. If each citizen is given two units of whatever is used as outside money in place of one, we should assume that the price level will more or less double. Or should we?

No, not really. Money can circulate at different speeds among households and firms, in particular if we refer to outside money. As we saw, there is no mechanical connection between supply and valuation, in particular for fiat money.

In complex monetary systems, where it is possible to write contracts based on the good used as monetary standard (inside money), the relation between the quantity of (outside) money and the price level (how much each unit of money can buy) is significantly less direct than one might imagine at first. It is important to understand that, as a matter of principle, one could economise on the use of the good used as money (tokens, gold coins, etc.) in a way that could validate *any* price level. Depending on the contract technology used to create inside money, one could sustain a monetary standard with close to no outside money at all (what is sometimes referred to as the 'cashless limit'). The amount of outside money available will therefore be immaterial to the determination of the price level.

Note, however, that the inside money equilibrium is fragile and in particular vulnerable to collapses in the confidence, by all market participants, that complete convertibility will be ensured. If such trust falls, the whole system might implode. Velocity falls precipitously and, unless it is compensated by increases in the supply of outside money (much more on this in Chapter 5), the price level may collapse. As we will see later, some authors use this mechanism to explain the most severe macroeconomic crisis of the last century, the Great Depression.

The relationship between the supply of physical goods that are used as money and the price level (i.e. the real value of that monetary asset) is therefore not a mathematical law, but rather a time-varying and unstable relationship that crucially depends on the substitutability between different forms of money that can be used as payment. Indeed, the quantity theory says that M★V = P★Y, the nominal amount of money M (for example, the number of gold coins in circulation) is equal to nominal spending (prices P multiplied by real income Y) but only taking into account V, the velocity of circulation. In the 'cashless limit', the velocity of circulation is infinite and any amount of spending can be sustained with negligible amounts of money. The quantity theory is therefore more an empirical question than a theory of the joint determination of money and prices, as is sometimes portrayed. If V absorbs all variation in M, there is no link between M and P. (Another important weakness of the quantity theory as a testable theory of prices is that M is not directly observable, as there are many different definitions of money.)

For example, Alex Cukierman of the University of Tel Aviv has compared the growth of central bank money (currency and bank reserves) during the hyperinflation in the Weimar Republic in 1921–1923 and in the United States during the global financial crisis. He computes points in time in which the expansion of that monetary aggregate is the same, in percentage terms, in 1921–1923 Germany and 2008 United States. He finds that in the latter episode the price level barely moved, while in the first case it had increased 15-fold! The difference between the two episodes is explained by the fact that the increase in central bank money was transformed into demand for goods and services in Weimar Germany, but hoarded by a liquidity-hungry financial sector in 2008.[15]

This is not to say that there is no link at all, empirically, between money growth and inflation. In fact, there is a lot of evidence that there is indeed a strong link, especially in the long run. Very high inflation can hardly happen without fast growth in any monetary aggregate. But the link is not automatic and is influenced by historical and institutional factors, as Cukierman rightly points out.

Monetary policy under commodity and fiat money

In a commodity based monetary system there is no real 'monetary policy' to speak of. Supply and demand for the commodity determines the price level and inflation. Essentially, the monetary policy decision available to policy-makers in a commodity based system like the Gold Standard is rather whether to maintain or suspend convertibility between banknotes and the commodity standard – and governments indeed abandoned or suspended convertibility many times, often in times of fiscal stress (wars). More than a deliberate policy, this was the result of political events beyond the economic and monetary sphere. Runaway inflation was typically the unavoidable consequence of abandoning convertibility.

In a fiat money system, we can see monetary policy also as a form of convertibility. In this case, convertibility refers to the value of central bank liabilities in terms of a broad basket of goods and services, at the (agreed by society) inflation target. As we will see in the next chapter, it is possible to interpret modern monetary policy and the Taylor principle (that we will also see there) as ways to operationalise this convertibility requirement. In fact, the late Fischer Black envisaged a monetary system based on convertibility between fiduciary (imaginary) money and a commodity, with near zero reserves, conducted just through open market operations (namely, market exchanges between central bank money and other assets).[16] Other authors have gone even further by imagining a monetary standard the value of which adjusts automatically to changes in the relative price of a broad basket of goods and services. We will come back to these schemes towards the end of the book.

A plan of the book

There is an enormous literature on central banking and in this book I had to make draconian choices in terms of content. The guiding principle is to empower the reader to follow the most important current debates surrounding central banking. This implies some time spent on principles, and some time on the open issues and debates themselves.

With that organising principle in mind, the book is organised in seven chapters, each dealing with a key open question on central banking.

We start with Chapter 2 which deals with the question of *how monetary policy works* and how it can control the price level and inflation. This chapter will review the logic of the 'mainstream' (New Keynesian) model of central bank action, based on inflation targeting and sticky prices (prices that are flexible in the long run but rigid in the short run), and will then discuss some plausible alternatives, such as price level targeting. We will argue that the reality of monetary policy implementation deviates substantially from the textbook version.

Chapter 3 mainly deals with questions related to *central bank independence*, which is taken for granted in the mainstream model. Why should central banks be independent? What evidence do we have that central bank independence helps? In this chapter I also discuss the relationship between the central bank and the government and the tension between monetary and fiscal dominance as a theory of the determination of the price level. The chapter will conclude that monetary or fiscal dominance are both possible depending on prevailing institutional and political factors. In this chapter, we also address two other complications to the mainstream model and show why they are important to understand monetary policy in practice – in particular, I will argue that the implementation of monetary policy is quite different from that described in textbook models.

Chapter 4 deals with the problem of the *zero bound* on interest rates. Because there is a risk free asset in the economy with zero nominal return, cash, nominal interest rates cannot go (very) negative. At times, this can be a significant constraint on monetary policy. The chapter will review the ways that have been suggested to eliminate or alleviate the zero bound problem, including non-standard monetary policies such as Quantitative Easing (QE).

Chapter 5 deals with the role of the *lender of last resort* (LOLR) of central banks. This has traditionally been one of the most important functions of central banks, which certainly predates the pursuit of price stability. Beyond reviewing the key reasons why a LOLR function is needed and beneficial, the chapter focuses on its optimal implementation, on ways to deal with moral hazard and finally on a few open questions, such as whether LOLR should be granted to non-bank financial intermediaries and governments.

Chapter 6 asks the question whether the *disappearance of paper currency* in favour of e-money and the like would prevent central banks from having any control on interest rates and the economy (the so-called 'cashless limit'). The chapter concludes that cash disappearance is both unlikely and would anyway probably not represent a serious problem for the implementation of monetary policy.

Chapter 7 turns to open economy questions and asks whether we will have a *world central bank and currency*, maybe in the distant future. We will first review pros and cons of flexible exchange rates and the external adjustment mechanisms under different exchange rate regimes (peg or float). The chapter then concludes that a global central bank is not likely because there is much more to central banking than an exchange rate arrangement. Moreover, I argue that the experience of the euro area (one central bank for many different sovereigns) will be crucial for whether and in what shape a global central bank will ever be introduced.

Finally, Chapter 8 deals with the most controversial question, namely if *we can or should do without central banks altogether*. It reviews claims by Friedrich Hayek and others that we should eliminate the monopoly of government-produced money and move towards currency competition and free provision of monetary services. Would we gain from more 'monetary entrepreneurship' and innovation in the monetary sphere? In this context, the chapter also describes strengths and weaknesses of digital currencies such as bitcoin. Its conclusion – which in a way is also the conclusion of the whole book – is that while central banks are highly unlikely to be replaced in the near future, they are in a constant state of evolution and they are unlikely to remain the same in future decades. We will conclude that we are not at the 'end of history' for central banking.

Notes

1 van der Cruijsen, C., Jansen, D. and J. de Haan, 'How Much Does the Public Know about the ECB's Monetary Policy? Evidence from a Survey of Dutch Households', *International Journal of Central Banking* 11, 4, 2015, 169–218.

2 Jost, A., 'Is Monetary Policy too Complex for the Public? Evidence from the UK', SNB Working Paper 15/2017.
3 One widely quoted earlier book on central banks is C. A. E. Goodhart, 'The evolution of central banks', MIT Press, 1988.
4 For this reason, saying that money is a financial asset, as sometimes done in the literature, is not very helpful, because money rather *defines* what a financial asset is.
5 Kiyotaki, N. and J. Moore, 'Evil is the Root of all Money', 2001, Clarendon Lectures 1.
6 Kocherlakota, N., 'Money is Memory', *Journal of Economic Theory*, 81, 2, 1996, 232–251. A similar point was made earlier by Ostroy and Starr, who wrote that 'money is a device to record and make public one's trading history'; see H. I. Grossman, 'Monetary Economics: A Review Essay', NBER Working Paper No. 3686, 1991.
7 Kindleberger, C., *Manias, Panics, and Crashes: A History of Financial Crises*, Basingstoke: Macmillan, 1978.
8 Dang, T. V., Gorton, G. and B. Holmström, 'The Information Sensitivity of a Security', mimeo, 2015, available at http://www.columbia.edu/~td2332/Paper_Sensitivity.pdf.
9 Mehrling, P., 'The Inherent Hierarchy of Money', 2012, available at http://ieor.colum bia.edu/files/seasdepts/industrial-engineering-operations-research/pdf-files/Mehrling_P_ FESeminar_Sp12-02.pdf.
10 See McKinnon, R., 'The Rules of the Game: International Money in Historical Perspective', *Journal of Economic Literature*, XXXI, 1993, 1–44.
11 See Rockoff, H., 'The "Wizard of Oz" as a Monetary Allegory', *Journal of Political Economy*, 98, 4, 739–760.
12 Because of the increased demand for gold, the last 30 years of the 19th century were mostly a period of deflation; see Barsky, R. and J. B. De Long, 'Forecasting Pre-World War I Inflation: The Fisher Effect and the Gold Standard', *Quarterly Journal of Economics*, 106, 3, 1991, 815–836, who find that gold mining forecasts inflation in 1879–1913. A tendency to deflation was often not seen as a major problem at the time (unlike today), because prices were mostly flexible at the time and growth was generally robust, at least until World War I. We will come back later more extensively to this argument.
13 Including death and mutilation in many countries.
14 Sargent, T. J. and F. R. Velde, *The Big Problem of Small Change*, Princeton: Princeton University Press, 2003.
15 Cukierman, A., 'Money Growth and Inflation: Policy Lessons from a Comparison of the US since 2008 with Hyper-inflation Germany in the 1920s', *Economics Letters* 54, 2017, 109–112; and private correspondence.
16 McCallum, B., 'Alternatives to the Fed?', *Cato Journal*, 30, 3, 2010.

2
HOW MONETARY POLICY WORKS
The mainstream model

In a commodity money standard, the price level is determined by the value of the commodity, or bundle of commodities, used for exchange. That value, in turn, is influenced both by the demand for and supply of that particular commodity. Governments can impose an official value to commodity based monies and have frequently done so, but typically they are sooner or later constrained by the intrinsic value of the metal (or the relative values, in case of a bimetallic standard).

For fiat money issued by central banks, instead, it makes sense to speak of monetary policy. We can define monetary policy as the regulation of the quantity of money, or its characteristics, in order to achieve a certain macroeconomic objective, e.g. keeping its real value relatively stable over time, which is desirable in a wide class of models. Because fiat money is government issued, monetary policy is the responsibility of a public institution, the central bank.

Note that we can also interpret monetary policy in a fiat money system as a form of convertibility. The objective of monetary policy can often be defined as maintaining convertibility between fiat money and a basket of goods and services, say the consumer price index (CPI). For example, the value of a monetary standard relative to the CPI should be stable. After all, this is what price stability is about.

In this chapter we will see how monetary policy is carried out in an analytical framework which I will caricature as "mainstream" and which has underpinned the relative success of monetary policy since the early 1980s.[1] The relative success is measured by the fact that, between the early 1980s and the global financial crisis in 2007–09, both inflation and real growth have been remarkably stable, a trend commonly dubbed as the Great Moderation. To be clear, the analytical approach that I will describe is not the 'cause' of the Great Moderation but more a way of thinking about monetary policy that has underpinned and rationalised central bank behaviour during it. If there is a single 'cause' for the Great Moderation, it has to be the Volcker dis-inflation in the United States, namely the attempt by the then-Chairman of the Federal Reserve Board, Paul Volcker, to stamp out inflation using monetary policy – and even that would probably be a stretch. However, that success has been made considerably more sustained and durable by a common way of thinking about the role of monetary policy that the mainstream model encapsulates. A good part, though not all, of this consensus has also survived the global financial crisis of 2007–09.

The mainstream model is also built on the assumption that central banks can focus on achieving price stability because they are independent and this is their main mandate. It is therefore an expression of a world in which 'monetary dominance' prevails. In the next chapter, we will see that this assumption is far from innocuous, or realistic everywhere and all the time.

Exit Bretton Woods, enter fiat money

Most of us, especially the young, may be forgiven for thinking that the current monetary system, based on inconvertible fiat money, is the only possible one, at least in modern times. We would probably see the Gold Standard as something remote, 'barbaric' and belonging to an uncivilised past. However, it is useful to pause and consider that we are living in an entirely fiat money system only since the early 1970s when the US, under the Nixon administration, decided to 'pull the plug' on the Bretton Woods system, which, in theory at least, linked the US dollar to gold. What looks like normal today is in fact quite extraordinary when seen from an historical point of view.

The beginning of the fiat money system was not very auspicious. Also under the influence of two large oil shocks in 1973 and 1979, the 1970s were a period of slowing growth and high and variable inflation – a period in fact dubbed as the Great Inflation. There is a fair amount of research on why central banks were not able to deliver stable prices during that period. One theory, mostly associated with Athanasios Orphanides at the Massachusetts Institute of Technology and co-authors, is that central banks misrepresented the underlying strength of the economy.[2] They believed that low growth, especially in the early 1970s, was due to cyclical factors and did not see the more permanent slowdown of productivity growth that was happening before their eyes. In order to support growth, they therefore chose a very expansionary monetary policy which only created more inflation. Another theory, mostly associated with the work of Edward Nelson at the Federal Reserve Board, is that policymakers did not see the link between monetary policy and inflation at all, and believed that other factors, such as cost push shocks, were decisive to explain high inflation.[3] Be it as it may, the man who stopped the Great Inflation was Paul Volcker, who 'just did it': he embarked on a tightening of US monetary policy which created a recession, may have cost the incumbent US president (Jimmy Carter) his job, and helped spark a couple of banking and financial crises at home and in Latin America, but he eventually succeeded in stamping out inflation.

More generally, if we consider that the world had never lived in an entirely fiat money system and that the beginning was so inauspicious, the Great Moderation period that followed, with its stable growth and low inflation, must be seen as a remarkable success. It was not at all obvious in, say, 1979 that a fiat monetary system was sustainable and could be successfully managed. On the whole, central banks have probably over-achieved in the past four decades, even with a global financial crisis to account for.

A very, very non-technical description of the mainstream approach

Before we delve into the more technical aspects of what I will call the mainstream approach, it is useful to give a simple and allegoric description to help the intuition. Surprisingly, I have not seen this being done in any other contribution that I know of. It is obviously a caricature, but it conveys the gist of the main story. It will hopefully allow you to explain modern monetary policy to your uncle – assuming that your uncle is not knowledgeable in monetary economics, of course. Readers who are already familiar with New Keynesian models may be offended by the simplicity of the description and can safely skip over the next few paragraphs.

At this point it is also useful to make a digression on models in economics. A model is essentially a simplification of reality that can give insight on one or at most a few key questions that are too complicated to address if all factors are considered. The model-builder therefore chooses to leave out some potentially relevant aspects in order to focus on the transmission channels that he or she believes to be most important for the problem at hand. If you want to forecast inflation next year, you can probably safely forget about quantum theory or the disappearance of the dinosaurs. But if you want to forecast inflation 30 years from now, probably some elements of history are useful and a broader set of factors needs to be considered. All models are therefore, strictly speaking, 'wrong'. It is therefore not a valid criticism of the mainstream model that it does not consider some element of how the economy actually works. For the model, for example, it is irrelevant whether, say, the utility that consumers derive from consumption really adds to their happiness or it is just manipulated by advertisement – a question that is of course very interesting in its own right. As long as their behaviour is reasonably in accordance with the prediction of the model along the dimension that matters (say, explaining inflation), we can leave this question out and focus on the key factors. If we succeed in doing that, then the model can be seen as useful, but still we cannot say that it is 'true'. A map, for example, can be useful even if it does not contain all details – in fact, a map as detailed as reality would be so large as to be useless.

Another useful digression concerns the concept of rational expectations that is a building block of modern equilibrium models. The New Keynesian model that we are describing in this chapter is, deep down, an equilibrium model in the tradition of the rational expectations revolution in economics, which took place in the 1970s led by economists such as Robert Lucas. One side effect of this revolution has been the increasing 'mathematisation' of economic models, which has made the modern economics literature quite inaccessible to the casual reader.

It is easy to caricature the most extreme version of this view, which says that economic agents (households and firms) always make the optimal decision in their allocation of time, spending, and so on. A simple talk with a friend or a neighbour, and indeed with yourself, suffices to convince us that human beings are not as rational as purported in these models – although, loosely speaking, observed behaviour also does not deviate entirely from the rational behaviour either, because people do act purposefully and following what they believe to be their own interest. Economics has responded to the challenge – there is an entire branch of literature called 'behavioural economics' that investigates exactly that question.[4] Nevertheless, it is important not to throw out the baby with the bath-water. A model assuming that agents act purposefully and in their own interest is a useful yardstick and a good starting point to understand more complex and realistic decision making, therefore it should not be dismissed out of hand. This is often a point of contention in discussions with acquaintances and friends who do not have an economics background.

A final important distinction to be made on models is that between 'reduced form' and 'structural' models. A simple example is perhaps the easiest way to convey the difference. If I see that it is likely to rain, I can bring with me an umbrella. A 'reduced form' model would note and measure a correlation between my taking an umbrella and subsequent rain. This is however not a structural model in the sense that it does not establish a chain of causation running from my taking the umbrella to the rain. The true structural model is, of course, a model where causality runs from the expectation of rain to my taking the umbrella. The reduced form model is vulnerable to the so-called 'Lucas critique' after Robert Lucas, who pointed this out first: you cannot take a correlation as a measure of the potential effect of a policy. For example, my taking or not taking an umbrella would have zero impact on the probability of rain (unless you really believe in Murphy's law), so the observed, reduced form correlation has no meaning as a guide for policy. The New Keynesian model – like the Real Business Cycle models on which it is based – claims to be structural, namely to uncover causal relationships – although the reader may not be surprised to hear that this, like almost everything else in economics, is also controversial. (Real Business Cycle models are models where households, firms and policy-makers are all rational and all markets clear, so that prices fully reflect preferences and technology. For example, the price of an apple reflects only how tasty it is for consumers and how difficult it is to grow.)

Armed with these necessary explanations and qualifications, let us consider a toy economy with a consumer (he) and a restaurant owner (she), who employs the consumer as cook. The restaurant owner derives profits from selling dinners and sets prices as a mark-up on marginal costs, which in her case is given by the wage she gives to the cook. The consumer can neither save nor borrow, and has to be convinced to do so by the level of the real interest rate (the real interest rate is the difference between the nominal interest rate and expected inflation; for example, if the nominal interest rate is 3% and inflation is 1%, the real interest rate is 2%). On the price setting, there is an optimal level of mark-up of prices over costs (say, the price is 20% higher than the marginal cost, implying a mark-up of 20%) which maximises the owner's profits: too much of it and the consumer will go elsewhere, but a bit of mark-up is ok as long as it is costly for the consumer to change restaurant (this assumption is called 'monopolistic competition'). Moreover, the restaurant owner cannot adjust the price of dinners immediately, but only with some delay, perhaps because he needs time to adjust the menus (this is called 'sticky prices').

The consumer finds it easier to pay with paper currency, issued by the central bank and carrying a zero nominal interest rate. He therefore has a demand for cash which is an inverse function of the nominal interest rate (more precisely the difference between the level of the interest rate and the interest rate paid by cash, which is zero). This is called the 'LM curve' in the model and allows the central bank to manipulate the nominal interest rate. (If this seems tricky to understand, it's also because it is one weak spot of the theory!)

The consumer decides his allocation of working time and consumption depending on the real interest rate – if it is high (low), he prefers to save more (less) and consume less (more). The extent to which he adjusts his consumption over time depends on how impatient he is (this is called in the model the 'Euler equation' after the Basel-born great mathematician Leonhard Euler). If he has a high urge for current consumption, he will want to consume more now and because he cannot borrow, he has to work harder. It turns out that it is difficult to empirically confirm the Euler equation, and this is a major puzzle in macroeconomics – especially so because this relationship is crucial for our understanding of how monetary policy works.[5]

Here's how our central bank can influence inflation, say on the upside. The central bank makes a cash transfer to the consumer, which makes him more willing to spend because it sends the interest rate down via the money demand curve (he is more 'satiated' with outside money). This pushes up the nominal interest rate, and as a result the agent wants to consume and work more. However, if the owner wants to have the consumer (now turned cook) work longer hours she has to pay him more (this is called 'Phillips curve' in the model), which increases her costs and reduces her mark-up below the level she wants. Over time, the owner will want to push prices up in order to restore the optimal mark-up and her profits. This creates inflation, until the mark-up reaches the desired level.

In this world, what should the central bank do? Essentially the task of the central bank is to keep inflation stable which also means that consumption and the mark-up are close to what respectively the consumer and the restaurant owner want. In the best of possible worlds, there is a 'divine coincidence' between keeping prices stable and real economic outcomes. This requires that the central bank 'knows' what is optimal for the consumer and the producer – but also that observing inflation is all we need to know if we are deviating from the optimal level.

After this admittedly simplistic account of the mainstream model, I now turn to explain its main building blocks.

The LM curve: money demand

The first essential building block of the mainstream approach is that there is a well-defined money demand function which has a negative relationship with the nominal interest rate, which is the opportunity cost of holding money as opposed to non-monetary short-term assets. Note that, in reality, the interesting variable from the standpoint of monetary policy implementation is bank reserves (outside money held by commercial banks), not currency in circulation (banknotes in the hands of the public), which is used mostly for small (or illegal) transactions and has low or near-zero interest rate elasticity.

In theory, in the absence of shocks and uncertainty controlling the price level and maintain 'convertibility' between outside money and a basket of goods and services at a predetermined price level (or inflation rate) should be very easy. If there is a well-defined demand for outside money and if the (nominal) amount of transactions depends on the availability of outside money then the monetary authority can provide exactly as much outside money so as to validate any price level it wants. The demand for money can be defined in real terms, say:

$$M/P = f(Y,R)$$

where M is outside money, P is the price level, Y is real income, and R is the nominal interest rate. Assuming that Y and R are given, it is sufficient to identify the value for M which validates any desired level of P. This is a simple solution that is typically associated with the name of Don Patinkin, who wrote about it in the 1950s.

In practice, things are significantly more complicated because money demand is too unstable due to financial innovation and other factors. For this reason, central banks prefer to control inflation through interest rates, not through monetary targeting – in fact, the 'Patinkin solution' to price level determinacy has been to a large extent forgotten, although in principle it is still an available option today.

At the same time, control of inflation through interest rates is more indirect and more complex than the Patinkin solution, as we will soon see. Some economists are even convinced that inflation *cannot* be controlled via interest rates only, although the historical record seems to strongly suggest otherwise.

We should also clarify at the outset that the starting level of the price index is not an interesting variable and we can take it as essentially given. Hence we are assuming that the price level at time $t-1$ is predetermined. The price level is a matter of convention in terms of the unit of measurement or order of magnitude in which it is defined. We could multiply all prices by a factor of 1000 and adopt a new currency worth one-thousandth of the old one and nothing would change, in principle. This is in fact what happened with the introduction of the euro, which led to a re-denomination of the price level. Again one could think, in abstract terms, that this would depend on the supply of outside money, but in reality it is more the other way round: it is rather the price level that determines the amount of outside money in circulation. Therefore, when we speak about the determination of the price level we intend the path of increase or decrease in the price level between now and the future, i.e. current and future inflation. Therefore, when speaking about price level determinacy we are talking about the evolution of the price level given the $t-1$ level, and it is thus equivalent to express things in terms of the price level or the inflation rate from t onwards.

Having clarified this important point, let us focus on the determination of the price level when the central bank wants to use the interest rate as the main policy instrument, using the money supply only as a way to control the interest rate. We will start with the case of flexible prices and then move to sticky prices (fixed in the short term and flexible in the long term).

Price level determination under flexible prices

Under flexible prices (i.e. prices that are free to move following fundamentals, say demand and supply), the controllability of inflation can be best understood using a simple 'core' model, consisting of these three equations:

$$R_t = r + E_t \pi_{t+1}$$

$$R_t = r + \varphi_\pi \pi_t$$

$$m_t = -\beta R_t$$

The first equation is the Fisher equation, which describes the relationship between the nominal interest rate R, the real interest rate r, and expected inflation (E is the expectation operator and π is inflation); the second equation is a policy rule for the central bank (the interest rate as a function of inflation); and the third equation is a simplified (outside) money demand equation, which says that the nominal interest rate can be influenced by varying m by inverting money demand (the details of how this can be done are less important for now). Because prices are flexible and there are no other distortions, we are assuming that r is given, determined by real factors outside the control of the central bank, such as tastes (say, the degree of impatience of consumers) and technology.

In words, the mainstream model can be expressed in this way:

Nominal interest rate = real interest rate + expected inflation (Fisher equation)
Nominal interest rate is a positive function of inflation (Policy rule)
Real money demand is a negative function of the nominal interest rate (Money demand)

For example, suppose the central bank decides to increase the (real) money supply m. Because cash is abundant, agents do not demand a lot of it at the margin, leading to a fall in its price. If we assume that the nominal rate of return on outside money is zero, this means that the nominal interest rate (the rate at which cash today is exchanged for cash tomorrow) has to fall. A lower nominal interest rate implies, from the Fisher equation, lower inflation expectations. But this does not allow us to conclude anything on the price *level* today or tomorrow; for example, it could be that the price level rises today, and goes back to the initial level in the future, or any other constellation of current and future price levels. Without making further assumptions on the policy rule, the system is *indeterminate* (there is an infinite number of price paths consistent with the three equations shown above).

In particular, pegging the nominal interest rate at a certain level, without regard to the inflation rate, is a recipe for price level indeterminacy. Central banks cannot just say: from now on, the interest rate will be 3% at all times. Mathematically, this conclusion can be seen by solving forward the simple model above for inflation. But the broader message is that it is not possible to fix something that is fundamentally real (the price level as the inverse of the real price of money) with something nominal (the nominal interest rate).

The Taylor principle

It is well known that the system allows only one determinate solution at zero inflation if the 'Taylor principle' applies, i.e. if the policy rule is such that $\varphi_\pi > 1$.[6] (A 'determinate solution' means that the system of equations has only one solution satisfying all equations.) To be precise, there is only one *non-explosive* solution, as all other solutions imply an explosive inflation rate. The Taylor principle implies inflation determinacy – up to an implausible explosive solution which is typically ruled out. The name 'Taylor principle' mainly comes from a 1993 paper by John Taylor and his subsequent work, where he suggested that a stabilising policy rule should foresee a reaction of the nominal interest rate to inflation with a coefficient larger than one.[7]

The Taylor principle is an expression of *monetary dominance*, i.e. the idea that inflation can be pinned down using monetary policy and monetary policy alone. This is, however, not the only theory of the determination of the price level, nor has this theory been prevalent and widespread in the past, as we will see in the next chapter.

One interesting interpretation of the Taylor principle is that it makes the expected (real) return on fiat money – the opportunity cost of holding it – indexed to inflation, which is a necessary condition for ensuring determinacy. The indexation to inflation ensures, in a way, a degree of convertibility into a basket of goods and services – i.e. something real, which in my opinion echoes the spirit, if not the letter, of the 'real bills' doctrine that we already saw in Chapter 1.

The rise of inflation targeting

Before the early 1980s it was far from being a widespread view that inflation can be effectively controlled by monetary policy and that, in the words of Milton Friedman, 'inflation is always and everywhere a monetary phenomenon'.[8] Various other theories of inflation determination circulated at the time. It was only after the Volcker disinflation in the United States that monetary policy came to be seen as the main means to control inflation. Economists and market participants have been like St. Thomas, they have first wanted to see the evidence before convincing themselves that inflation can be controlled by monetary policy.

Since the 1980s a kind of 'doctrine' has established itself which can be summarised as inflation targeting, which guides central banks around the world. Inflation targeting is a monetary policy strategy which subordinates monetary policy to the achievement of a numerical target for inflation within a certain time horizon. To a large extent, inflation targeting is still the main paradigm for central banks even after the global financial crisis of 2007–09.

Inflation targeting is not a revolutionary phenomenon but rather a useful refinement of previous ideas and policies by central banks. In fact, if they are highly successful at inflation targeting there will be no need to apply the Taylor principle at all. Because inflation is well anchored, it will not rise or fall (apart from temporary factors) in the first place, which makes the application of the Taylor principle almost impossible to see.

The key elements of this doctrine are four. First, inflation can be controlled by monetary policy (monetary dominance). Second, central banks should be given the task of controlling inflation through a numerical target, which also provides clarity to economic agents, and makes central banks accountable. In advanced countries the numerical target is often 2%. Third, central banks should be left alone to pursue this goal away from short-term (and election-induced) political interference (central bank independence). Fourth, central banks can deliver on their mandate of delivering target inflation if they follow some version of the Taylor principle. This doctrine has generally worked very well at least until the global financial crisis of 2007–09; inflation has been low and stable in most advanced countries and in many emerging countries as well. We will see later how and why keeping inflation low and stable is a desirable goal of economic policy.

It is not clear who 'invented' inflation targeting as such, but the first country to formally introduce it was New Zealand in the Reserve Bank Act of 1989. Frederic Mishkin at Columbia University provides an historical record of the evolution of inflation targeting and of how it conquered the central banking world in the 1980s and 1990s.[9] Recent research points out that inflation targeting does not lead to more stable and controllable inflation as such, while they could be both determined by a third factor, such as the quality of the institutions.[10]

Sticky prices

So far, we have looked at price determinacy without regard to whether zero inflation is optimal in any way. Indeed, in a world with flexible prices and flexible markets the choice of the inflation target does not really matter much. With sticky prices, instead, monetary policy plays an important stabilisation role which matters for agents' welfare. Let us see how.[11]

By sticky prices we typically mean that changing prices is costly, and hence firms tend to minimise changes. Eventually, prices will converge to their equilibrium level (i.e. the one prevailing under flexible prices), but in the short term they are more likely to remain fixed.

There are several competing explanations as to why prices are sticky. One explanation is menu costs, i.e. the physical cost of changing price signs – but prices are even sticky online to some extent,[12] which seems to contradict this explanation. A second explanation is 'rational inattention', i.e. the idea that firms do not pay attention to prices unless they are very much out of line with optimal prices. Explanations based on 'sticky information' emphasise the possibility that firms may not have up to date information on the fundamentals that are needed for updating prices – say, marginal costs or prices of competitors. Finally, especially increasing prices may be seen as unfair by consumers, and there is evidence for this tendency, although also this is not a complete explanation since prices appear to be sticky both on the upside (where fairness should matter more) and on the downside (where it should matter less). Wages do seem to be more rigid downwards, perhaps because wage earners are for some reason particularly averse to nominal cuts, but again the evidence is not universal.

Irrespective of the reason behind the fact that prices are sticky, what changes under sticky prices compared with flexible prices? Sticky prices and wages imply that the economy behaves like a flexible price economy in the long run, but prices and wages are fixed in the short run. This implies that (i) relative prices may be distorted, if prices and wages are adjusted at different times, and (ii) at a macro level, the relative price of tomorrow's vs. today's consumption may also be distorted, meaning that the real interest rate deviates from the value it would take under fully flexible prices. In other words, sticky prices distort the inter-temporal allocation of economic activity and consumption. For example, the real interest would be lower than the level implied by, say, time preference, leading to an inefficient boom in consumption and economic activity.

The mainstream model is called 'New Keynesian' because prices are fixed in the short term (this is the supposedly Keynesian part), but it is also 'new' because, unlike Keynesian economics, it is based on micro-foundations and rational expectations and, at its core, it is a Real Business Cycle model, where agents have rational expectations and optimise their choices.

In the New Keynesian frame of thinking the main task of monetary policy is to remove this distortion and to try and set the economy as close as possible to the flexible price equilibrium trajectory. In other words, central banks should make sure that distortions arising from sticky prices hurt as little as possible.

There is indeed quite ample evidence that prices are sticky; the degree of stickiness is also likely to be shock dependent.[13] There is also substantial evidence that the degree of price stickiness is endogenous to the monetary policy regime; it is higher when inflation is low and stable, when households and firms do not expect large price adjustments, and lower when inflation is high. Under hyperinflation prices are typically very flexible and change by the day and even by the hour. There appears to be an equilibrating factor at play: high and variable inflation amplifies the distortions due to sticky prices, but prices are also less sticky if inflation is high and volatile, as if the economy was 'protecting itself' from excessive distortions.

Prices also tend to be changed in a seasonal way, for example in January. Evidence of nominal wage rigidity, in particular downward rigidity (wage earners resent nominal wage cuts, in particular), is also substantial. Finally, there is evidence that prices are stickier in Europe than in the US.[14]

The sticky price basic model

How does the little model that we have seen so far change if sticky prices are introduced?

The standard New Keynesian model under sticky prices may be described by these three equations:

$$y_t = E_t y_{t+1} - \sigma(R_t - E_t \pi_{t+1}) + d_t$$

$$R_t = r + \varphi_\pi \pi_t$$

$$\pi_t = \beta E_t \pi_{t+1} + k(y_t - y_t^*) + s_t$$

where y is output, and y★ is the flexible price level of output. The first equation is a standard Euler equation for output (normally it is defined for consumption), the second equation is a policy rule as in the simplified model seen earlier, and the third equation is a forward looking Phillips curve determining inflation. In particular, inflation now depends on the difference between actual and flexible price level of output, i.e. the output gap, namely $y_t - y_t^*$. The 'output gap' is a term that is very fashionable in central banking, and you hear it often in conferences and policy discussions. Intuitively, an output gap means that the economy is either 'too hot' or 'too cold', namely there is either too much or too little of economic activity.

As a result of sticky prices, the real interest rate (the term in parentheses in the Euler equation) deviates from the flexible price equilibrium, giving rise to a 'real interest rate gap'. In turn, the Euler equation determines the link between the output gap and the real interest rate gap. Under fully flexible prices, of course, the output gap and the real interest rate gap disappear.

The shocks *d* and *s* are respectively aggregate demand and supply shocks. In general demand shocks are unexpected shifts in aggregate demand, for example because households are more optimistic about the future and want to spend more. In most models, this results in a positive shift in both production and prices. Supply shocks are unexpected improvements in the economy's productive capacity, for example the invention or adoption of a new machine; these shocks tend to increase income but decrease prices, and from this characteristic they can be distinguished from demand shocks. (Unexpected shifts in monetary policy can also be seen as demand shocks.)

For the central bank, it is typically easier to deal with demand shocks, because they move output and inflation in the same direction and can be fully offset by monetary policy (i.e. by changes in R). This is what the literature calls the 'divine coincidence'. Supply shocks, however, are more complicated to deal with, and changes in R will normally be unable to completely eliminate fluctuations in inflation and the output gap — in particular, zero inflation and output gap cannot be achieved simultaneously.

Described in words, the model says:

Consumption = Tomorrow's expected consumption − real interest rate (Euler equation)
Inflation = Tomorrow's expected inflation + f(Current consumption − flexible price consumption) (Phillips curve)
Nominal interest rate as a positive function of inflation (Policy rule)
Real money demand as a negative function of the nominal interest rate (Money demand)

Note that I have highlighted in italics the equations that we saw already in the flexible price version of the model. The first equation is also there in the flexible price version, but it is an equilibrium condition that does not matter for monetary policy, while it becomes important in the sticky price version. The second equation, the Phillips curve (which takes its name from Bill Phillips, a New Zealand economist who taught at the London School of Economics and first discovered the relationship), is new and is only there in the sticky price version; it says that inflation is driven by the difference between actual consumption and the equilibrium level that would prevail under flexible prices.

Compared with standard flexible-price, Real Business Cycle (RBC) models, New Keynesian models contain two key frictions, namely (i) monopolistic competition and (ii) sticky prices. Monopolistic competition implies that prices are set as a mark-up over marginal costs and they are not entirely determined by the latter. For example, a restaurant may charge higher prices than the marginal cost (which would prevail under perfect competition) counting on the fact that it would be costly for clients to change — say, the next restaurant is not next door or is less known by the consumer. If the restaurant charges outrageous prices, however, it will lose clients, so there is an optimal level of mark-up and firms will try to establish this level as much as possible. If updating prices is costly, a rise in marginal costs (say, due to a boom in economic activity[15]) will temporarily compress the mark-up below the equilibrium level; over time, the right mark-up level will be restored through inflation. This means that profit margins are too low in good times, and too high in bad times.

Monetary policy under sticky prices

As mentioned, in a New Keynesian setting optimal monetary policy should minimise the sticky price distortion and try to replicate the flexible price equilibrium.[16]

In terms of the transmission channels, in a New Keynesian model the central bank either starves or floods the economy with outside money, notably bank reserves. This influences its price (the nominal interest rate). Due to sticky prices, this in turn influences the real interest rate through the Fisher equation (note that it would not under flexible prices). Through the Euler equation, there will be inefficient fluctuations in consumption and investment, which will affect marginal costs and drive inflation with some lag in the Phillips curve. In the long term, the model behaves exactly like a flexible price model with full neutrality of money (namely, where money only determines nominal variables, and no real variable).

Which price index should the central bank target?

Under inflation targeting, what price index should the central bank target? Traditionally, it is believed that it is optimal for the central bank to target the sticky price section of the consumer price basket. Things are more complicated if wages are also sticky; and in fact it is likely that any meaningful aggregate used for inflation targeting should in principle also include wages.[17] However, most countries target a wide measure of the consumer price index because it is rightly believed to be more representative of consumer spending. It would not make much sense for consumers to know that sticky price inflation is stable, if the flexible part is out of control. At the same time, this common sense consideration seems to be outside, and not necessarily in keeping with, the mainstream model where the key distortion to be eliminated is given by sticky prices. This is an area where there is an unresolved discrepancy between theory and policy.

Some economists even argue that not only the price of durable goods, but also some asset prices (housing prices, in particular, are often not included in the CPI or included only marginally) should be included in the price index used for inflation targeting – an idea originally proposed by Alchian and Klein in the early 1970s.[18] First, some asset prices may also be sticky like other prices (e.g., housing prices). Second, these prices are representative of the agents' consumption basket (assets are deferred consumption in the future, after all). Third, it can even be claimed that including some asset prices in the price index on which the inflation target is based would be a way for monetary policy to effectively 'lean against the wind' and prevent booms and busts in credit and asset prices, and their repercussions for financial stability (see Chapter 5). This is the so-called 'macro-prudential reason' to include property prices in the inflation target, but it is disputed whether this would really help maintain financial stability.

The definition of the price index that the central bank targets is an intriguing topic, which is worthy of more attention than it currently receives – I often hear people saying that it is easy to define price stability, but this is not really true. Generally speaking, central banks are wary of targeting asset prices because of the larger role of speculative factors and the difficulty of controlling those prices via interest rates. But in my opinion the question of whether asset prices should be included in a measure of the consumer price index remains wide and open. It is not obvious to the layman that, for example, the fridge in the kitchen is in the price index targeted by central banks, but the house which hosts it mostly is not.[19]

Limitations of inflation targeting

As noted, inflation targeting is a somewhat narrow view of central banking, which however has the advantage of being well developed, internally consistent and clear. It is therefore a good benchmark to understand and guide monetary policy. At the same time, clearly there are several important elements which are missing in New Keynesian models. Financial stability and booms/busts in credit and asset prices come in the first place in the list, and this shortcoming became painfully evident during the global financial crisis. We will see this in much more detail in Chapter 5.

The mechanism of inflation expectations creation is straightforward in New Keynesian models (rational expectations) but not very realistic and not always supported by the data. In practice we see that inflation expectations are either (too) well anchored and consumers are naïve (they expect inflation to remain at the central bank target no matter what) or, conversely, they may deviate from the target for no clear or apparent reason. More generally, it is often difficult to regain control of inflation expectations once it has been lost. This is even more so after deflationary expectations become entrenched, as shown by the Japanese experience of the last two decades that we will see in more detail in Chapter 4.

Finally, there are other important costs of inflation that are often not incorporated in the mainstream model – where all the cost of inflation comes from the sticky price distortion. For example, inflation uncertainty has an important negative effect on economic activity, and the level and volatility of inflation are normally positively correlated. Very high inflation is disruptive in particular for financial intermediation, which is still often based on nominal contracts. This is especially evident during hyper-inflation episodes. There is even evidence that monetary instability undermines the rule of law.[20]

Very high inflation, and hyper-inflation (very high and explosive inflation) are very disruptive phenomena, which can wreak havoc on economies, in particular by hindering trade, damaging or destroying financial intermediation and long-term contracts, and by contributing to abrupt income redistribution and a general lack of cohesion and security. Often, these phenomena are associated with, and in part also contribute to, social unrest and upheaval.[21] Moreover, very high inflation is often associated to a dysfunctional State, for example in the area of tax collection or budgeting process.

The economic structure of countries can adapt to high inflation to some extent, but not to the point of making it harmless. For example, prices become more flexible, the length of contracts shortens, and so forth. Multiple standards can arise: spot markets for long lasting assets are dollarised (i.e. based on widespread use of foreign currency), housing and wages are indexed to inflation, and retail markets in domestic money.[22] Generally speaking, economic performance under hyper-inflation is far worse than with monetary stability.

Money illusion is also an important feature of the real world that is not sufficiently recognised in most macro models. The evidence clearly points to the fact that people are often not able to understand the real value of goods and services and they focus on the monetary value, namely the value expressed in units of money.[23] As soon as price is 'framed' in a particular unit or currency, that unit is used almost automatically as a measure of value. Again, this squares well with my casual and anecdotal evidence, and economists are certainly not completely immune to this tendency.

Distributional aspects may also be important for monetary policy. Generally speaking, the poor are less protected against inflation, so keeping inflation low and stable is beneficial for social cohesion and political stability. In fact, political instability and high inflation are often associated, although the direction of causality is not clear.

The fact that all these elements are not included in the New Keynesian baseline model is not necessarily a problem, because they are largely consistent with its main message, namely that it is desirable to keep inflation low and stable. To a large extent, they just provide an additional justification to the policy implications. However, the transmission channels may be different, and the optimal policy may to some extent depart from the one identified with the mainstream New Keynesian model, although I am not aware of a systematic exploration of this question.

Why a positive inflation target, rather than zero?

A final question on inflation targeting would be: Why not zero inflation? Why do most central banks target 2% rather than zero inflation?

In terms of welfare, there is probably little difference between zero and 2% inflation. In both cases inflation does not feature prominently in economic decisions, which is a relevant definition of price stability after all. In fact, there is plenty of evidence that high inflation is negative for economic growth, but the evidence is not clear-cut for moderate inflation. While 100% inflation is clearly bad for economic performance, the difference between, say, 2% or 4% inflation is small or perhaps non-existent.

There are a few valid reasons why 2% inflation may be better than zero inflation, although 2% is not a 'magic number' and is largely a convention. Quality improvement is a first reason. Goods and services improve over time and this is not fully reflected in price statistics (this is called 'hedonic improvement'). For example, the car I buy today may be very different from, and better than, the car I bought ten years ago, but still be recorded as a car in the price statistics.[24] As pointed out by Larry Summers at Harvard University, few of us would like to enjoy 1970 healthcare at 1970 prices, or for that matter a 1970 car at 1970 prices, which implies that there is at least some serious measurement error in the price statistics.[25] Targeting 2% rather than zero inflation helps to some extent to correct these statistical distortions.

Second, the higher the inflation target, the higher the average level of nominal interest rates (by virtue of the Fisher equation), which – for given size of the shocks hitting the economy – implies a lower probability of hitting the zero bound. Third, wages are rigid to the downside; a little inflation can allow more flexibility in real wages without requiring an adjustment in nominal wages.[26] Finally, positive average inflation allows different inflation rates at the regional level without requiring at least some regions to be in outright deflation. This is important, for example, in large countries and in a monetary union such as the euro area – otherwise we might see entire regions such as Northern or Southern countries in protracted deflation over time.

In conclusion, the New Keynesian approach is a useful analytical framework to think about monetary policy. As any model, it has some main shortcomings and three of them are noteworthy. First, it assumes that the central bank is in charge of price stability and is independent in its actions, namely that monetary dominance prevails. In history, however, the fiscal situation of the government exerts an important effect on monetary policy, and in some cases it has been dominant (fiscal dominance). The framework has not been used enough to understand interactions between fiscal and monetary policy. Second, although it is not a limitation of the model itself but more of the way it was used, central banks have not reflected enough on the role of the zero lower bound until interest rates became mostly stuck at the bound in the wake of the global financial crisis. Finally, the framework at least in its most classic specification does not give enough attention to financial factors and financial frictions, and is therefore not really suited to understand issues of financial stability and banking crises. This limitation too seemed immaterial in the world before the global financial crisis, but has come back to haunt central banks in 2007–2009. In the next three chapters, we will focus on each of these three main questions in turn.

Notes

1 A classic reference for the mainstream New Keynesian model is Gertler, M., Gali, J. and R. Clarida, 'The Science of Monetary Policy: A New Keynesian Perspective', *Journal of Economic Literature* 37, 4, 1999, 1661–1707.
2 Orphanides, A., 'The Quest for Prosperity without Inflation', *Journal of Monetary Economics*, 50, 3, 2003, 633–663.
3 Nelson, E., 'The Great Inflation of the Seventies: What Really Happened?', *The B. E. Journal of Macroeconomics*, 5, 1, 2005, 1–50.
4 In fact, the author of this book did his PhD dissertation exactly on behavioural economics.
5 See Stracca, L., 'The Euler Equation around the World', *B. E. Journal of Macroeconomics*, Advances, 17, 2, 2017, 1–9.
6 It is easy to generalise to any non-zero inflation target; zero inflation here is just a normalisation.

7 Taylor, J., 'Discretion versus Policy Rules in Practice', *Carnegie-Rochester Conference Series on Public Policy* 39, 1, 1993, 195–214.
8 Friedman, M., *Inflation Causes and Consequences*, New York: Asia Publishing House, 1963.
9 Mishkin, F., 'Inflation Targeting: True Progress or Repackaging of an Old Idea?', mimeo, 2006.
10 Dergiades, T., Milas, C, and T. Panagiotidis, 'An Assessment of the Inflation Targeting Experience', Eesti Pank Working paper series 11/2017, available at https://www.eestipank.ee/en/publications/series/working-papers.
11 A good reference for sticky prices in general and their importance for macroeconomics is Ball, L. and G. N. Mankiw, 'A Sticky-price Manifesto', *Carnegie-Rochester Conference Series on Public Policy* 41, 1, 1994, 127–151.
12 Arbatskaya, M. and M. R. Baye, 'Are Prices "Sticky" Online? Market Structure Effects and Asymmetric Responses to Cost Shocks in Online Mortgage Markets', *International Journal of Industrial Organization* 22, 10, 2004, 1443–1462.
13 Boivin, J., Giannoni, M. and I. Mihov, 'Sticky Prices and Monetary Policy: Evidence from Disaggregated US Data', *American Economic Review* 99, 1, 2009, 350–384.
14 See Alvarez, L., Dhyne, E., Hoeberichts, M., Kwapil, C., Le Bihan, H., Lünnemann, P., Martins, F., Sabbatini, R., Stahl, H., Vermeulen, P. and J. Vilmunen, 'Sticky Prices in the Euro Area: A Summary of New Micro-Evidence', *Journal of the European Economic Association* 4, 2–3, 2006, 575–584.
15 For example, if workers want to be paid more if they work longer hours.
16 Note that in most New Keynesian models the efficient stabilisation of relative prices results in a higher average mark-up, implying more distortions from monopolistic competition even in the steady state, namely in the long-term solution of the model. See Corsetti, G. and P. Pesenti, 'The Simple Geometry of Transmission and Stabilization in Closed and Open Economies', *NBER International Seminar on Macroeconomics*, 2007, 65–116.
17 See Mankiw, G. and R. Reis, 'What Measure of Inflation Should a Central Bank Target?', *Journal of the European Economic Association*, 1, 5, 2003, 1058–1086.
18 See Alchian, A. A. and B. Klein, 'On a Correct Measure of Inflation', *Journal of Money, Credit and Banking* 5, 1, 1973, 173–191. For a good survey see Goodhart, C., 'What Weight Should be Given to Asset Prices in the Measurement of Inflation?', *Economic Journal* 111, 2001, F335–56.
19 One additional argument for keeping house prices out of the CPI is that real estate is normally bought from other households, and therefore it is doubtful that an increase in prices affects all households in a similar way (as when, for example, the price of apples rises). Even this argument, however, is controversial.
20 Koyama, N. and B. Johnson, 'Monetary Stability and the Rule of Law', *Journal of Financial Stability* 17, 2014, 46–58.
21 Fischer, S., Sahay, R. and C. A. Vegh, 'Modern Hyper- and High Inflations', *Journal of Economic Literature* 40, 3, 2002, 837–880; Leijonhufvud, A., 'High Inflations and Contemporary Monetary Theory', University of California, Los Angeles Working Paper 638, 1991.
22 See Leijonhufvud (op. cit.).
23 Shafir, E., Diamond, P. and A. Tversky, 'Money Illusion', *Quarterly Journal of Economics* 112, 2, 1997, 341–374.
24 Note that statistical offices try to capture this phenomenon through the so-called 'hedonic adjustment', but probably not fully.
25 See Larry Summers' blog at http://larrysummers.com/2015/05/20/feldstein-argues-price-indices-underestimate-real-income-growth/.
26 The classic reference here is Akerlof, G., Dickens, W. R. and G. Perry, 'The Macroeconomics of Low Inflation', *Brookings Papers on Economic Activity* 27, 1, 1996, 1–76.

3

THREE QUESTIONS ON THE MAINSTREAM MODEL

In the previous chapter we have seen that the mainstream approach leads to a consistent framework in which central bankers have been thinking about monetary policy in the Great Moderation period. The fact that central banks have been collectively able to maintain price stability only two decades after the establishment of an entirely new monetary system, based on inconvertible fiat money, is a very significant success that should not be downplayed, and which could not be taken for granted in the 1970s. The mainstream approach has provided a fundamental intellectual foundation to the success of central banks in the practical task of maintaining price stability, at least in advanced countries. The fact that this has proven to be a useful analytical framework and that it has underpinned the Great Moderation does not imply, however, that all assumptions of the mainstream view are correct, nor that the underlying model is 'true'. Like any model or any simplification of the world, it is wrong in some respects, possibly many. And there are, in fact, at least three fundamental questions surrounding the mainstream approach. We are going to see each of them in turn in this chapter.[1]

Who controls the price level?

The first main problem of the mainstream approach is that it assumes that the central bank is ultimately in control of the money supply and hence of the price level. It views the monetary authority as an independent branch of government that it is entrusted with the task to deliver price stability, using all possible means to achieve it. That may correspond to the letter of the legal provisions in many countries nowadays, but, first, it has not been the law for most of the history of central banks and, second, it may not fully reflect the reality of central bank conduct even now.

Looking back at history, we have seen that central banks have been created with none of the characteristics that we normally associate with them today – they were in fact created as private institutions, often with the only 'macroeconomic' task of providing cheap financing to the government to finance wars. As Thomas Cargill at University of Nevada adequately put it, most central banks were at the origin a good example of crony capitalism. Central banks have not been created independent, they have become so over time. One possible exception is the Deutsche Bundesbank which was established in very special conditions, in 1948 by the Allied authorities which were occupying defeated Germany at the time. The Deutsche Bundesbank was modelled after the US Federal Reserve – although in fact at the time the Federal Reserve did not enjoy full independence from the executive. Of course, and largely reflecting the experience of the Bundesbank, the European Central Bank was also created, by the Maastricht Treaty in 1992, to be fully independent. On the whole, there is therefore nothing 'natural' or unavoidable that central banks are independent and focused on price stability.

Second, *de iure* central bank independence does not necessarily imply *de facto* independence. Central banks are ultimately a branch of government and it is quite likely that the political sphere exerts some influence on central bank decisions. The influence may be larger in certain conditions and countries than in others, but undoubtedly it is there. It is the parliament and the government who appoint central bank governors, a reality that undoubtedly current and prospective governors forget at their peril.[2] Central bank independence is a matter of degree, rather than a 'yes' or 'no' situation.

But do we really need central bank independence? The traditional view, which has many arguments in its favour, is that monetary policy needs to be run by an independent institution because it needs to have the right medium-term orientation, away from the political cycle and the need to be re-elected. If monetary policy were influenced by short-term considerations, it would try to excessively stimulate output, but over time the only result of this would be to have permanently higher inflation. In the literature this is seen as a manifestation of the 'time inconsistency' problem: I will not do tomorrow what I today think will be optimal. In daily life, for example, time inconsistency means shifting an unwanted obligation (say, going to the dentist) to the future, knowing too well that when the time comes we will find it optimal to postpone again.

This way to look at incentives for central banks over time is known as the 'Barro-Gordon' model of central bank independence.[3] A related, but different solution is offered by Ken Rogoff at Harvard University: to correct for the short-term bias toward growth, politicians should appoint a central banker who is more 'conservative' than they are, i.e. somebody who dislikes inflation more than they do.[4] Rogoff's solution is also interesting because it is the first to focus on the institutional aspect of central banking. Another main reason for central bank independence is that monetary policy is a technical matter requiring expertise that needs to be developed over time, away from the vagaries of the political cycle. This is obviously the case in many other professional activities, such as the police or justice, which are also shielded from the political process.

It is also important to distinguish between goal independence (the central bank sets its own objective) from instrument independence (the central bank chooses the instrument to achieve a goal given by somebody else). There is a consensus that goal independence is questionable, whereas instrument independence is important and useful. However, even instrument independence may have some limits which have been tested in the wake of the global financial crisis, when central banks have resorted to more and more unconventional policies. Are all means licit if the goal is a good one?

What does the evidence say? There is in fact a fair amount of empirical evidence that central bank independence (CBI) is correlated with low inflation. Can we therefore prevent fiscal dominance just by granting independence to central banks? Adam Posen at the Peterson Institute thinks that this is not the case, and the case for a causal link from central bank independence to inflation is illusory.[5] Both may depend on a common factor, namely the degree of inflation aversion in society, which simultaneously determines CBI and inflation outcomes.[6]

The fiscal theory of the price level

Some economists bring these considerations one step further and reason that, ultimately, fiat money is a government creation and cannot be produced in isolation from the government budget and its sustainability. This is commonly known as the fiscal theory of the price level. In simple terms, the reasoning goes more or less like this. The real value of today's public debt must be equal, by definition and barring default, to the discounted sum of all government primary surpluses in the future. (The primary surplus is the difference between government revenues and expenditure, net of interest expenses for servicing the debt.) Therefore, high public debt today implies a sequence of high expected primary surpluses tomorrow. In practice, this means a lot of (distortionary) taxes down the road, because public expenditure is difficult to reduce in the short term. Countries may reach their so-called 'fiscal limit': they cannot tax people more than a certain level without facing economic backlash (possibly even undermining tax revenues), political stability and social cohesion. Once a country is at the fiscal limit, primary surpluses cannot be increased any further.

But there is another variable that can influence the real value of public debt: inflation. Because public debt is held in nominal terms (more on the reasons for this in Chapter 5), surprise inflation typically reduces the real value of debt. Because central banks, again, are ultimately government agencies even when they are nominally independent, they will feel compelled to bend their rules and objectives in order to ensure that public debt is sustainable, so the view goes. In turn, this pins down the price level and inflation today, according to the fiscal theory. (More concretely, high public debt implies a high inflation regime, irrespective of what the central bank would want.)

Unpleasant monetarist arithmetic

In modern macroeconomics nothing happens without expectations, and here it is no exception. The story goes that, because agents anticipate the outcome of the government forcing the hand of the central bank, high public debt today already leads to high equilibrium inflation and hence high inflation expectations, even if the central bank is not, or not yet, an active accomplice. Hence, the fiscal situation of the government is a more relevant predictor of the price level than the central bank declared inflation target. One can even envisage a sort of 'self-fulfilling' fiscal dominance which develops in the following doomsday scenario: doubts about fiscal sustainability lead bond holders to expect the central bank to cave in and abandon its inflation target. This raises inflation expectations and leads to a spike in bond yields. The central bank initially sticks to its guns, with the unpleasant consequence of unduly increasing the *ex ante* real interest rate (nominal interest rate minus expected inflation). The government is now faced with high real financing costs, which jeopardise fiscal sustainability. Eventually it will exert enough pressure on the central bank to accommodate the public's expectations, validating the bondholders' initial view. In fact, one interesting corollary of the fiscal theory is that, under fiscal dominance, increasing interest rates to control inflation may be counterproductive, since the fall in inflation exaggerates the fiscal sustainability problem of the government, leading to more, not less inflation down the road. This is known as the 'unpleasant monetarist arithmetic' of Tom Sargent and Neil Wallace.[7]

A slightly more sophisticated version of the theory makes monetary or fiscal dominance state dependent. If public debt is sustainable (at least in the eyes of debt holders), monetary policy is independent of fiscal policy and focuses on price stability. In this case, we have monetary dominance. But as soon as fiscal sustainability is at risk, central banks increasingly pay attention to fiscal developments and fiscal considerations gradually or abruptly take over. Fiscal dominance is the result.

Active and passive fiscal policy

It is also useful to look at the interaction between monetary and fiscal policy from the standpoint of the fiscal policy-maker. Eric Leeper at Indiana University introduced a useful distinction between 'active' and 'passive' fiscal policies. The terminology is in fact slightly misleading because, perhaps counter-intuitively, the passive fiscal policy maker adapts its primary surplus (mostly taxes) to changes in monetary policy; it therefore ensures that the government intertemporal budget constraint (namely the constraint that government debt has ultimately to be paid back somehow) is satisfied for given monetary policy, i.e., current and expected inflation. The active policy-maker does the opposite: he refuses to take monetary policy as given and does not change the primary surplus as monetary conditions or fiscal sustainability evolve, perhaps because it is already at the fiscal limit. Fiscal dominance hence presupposes an 'active' fiscal policy in the sense given by Leeper, whereas monetary dominance requires a passive fiscal authority.[8]

One vocal supporter of the fiscal theory of the price level, John Cochrane at Stanford University, has argued that whether fiscal policy is active or passive has material consequences for the functioning of the standard New Keynesian model of the mainstream view. The foundation of this model, which we saw in the previous chapter, and its key conclusion for monetary policy, the Taylor principle, actually hold only if fiscal policy is passive. When fiscal policy is active in the sense of Leeper, the standard result is reversed: inflation is indeterminate if the central bank follows the Taylor principle, and is determinate otherwise.[9] (Recall that determinacy implies that the system of equations describing the economy has only one solution.) Of course, this also echoes the unpleasant monetarist arithmetic of Sargent and Wallace. What is useful to take away from this analysis is that any analysis of monetary policy cannot be made independently of a reaction of fiscal policy. And, in fact, this is an active area of research right now.

History is suggestive of the fact that monetary discipline and fiscal dominance alternate in time depending on circumstances, in particular whether the country is in a state of peace or war. In the United States, for example, price stability during the Gold Standard in peace time was replaced by inflation (driven by some monetisation of debt) in war times, when fiscal dominance tended to prevail.[10] In war times the US central bank, the Federal Reserve, has often been ready to suspend convertibility and bend itself to the financing needs of the government,[11] at least until the Accord during the Korean War with the Treasury in 1951, when it refused to continue monetary financing of the government debt (at least as an automatic policy). A similar development was the so-called 'divorzio' (divorce) between the Banca d'Italia and the Italian Treasury in 1981, when the central bank stopped having the obligation to purchase government bonds on the primary market. Like the Accord of 1951, this was more *de iure* than *de facto*, because the Banca d'Italia immediately started large scale purchases of government bonds in the secondary market. In many countries, governments have explicitly or implicitly asked the central bank to peg the interest rate on their liabilities. This is a typical expression of fiscal dominance, although it was also realised in other ways, notably through financial repression (namely by 'force feeding' government bonds to captive savers).

There are important advantages of using the printing press, that is inflation, to finance government deficits: these include low administrative costs, the possibility of largely hiding the true cost of war from citizens, and the fact that the 'wealth tax' (the redistribution from creditors to debtors) brought about by surprise inflation is widely distributed, as Benjamin Franklin had already pointed out during the American Revolution.[12] The widespread use of the monetisation option in history should therefore come as no surprise.

Does the fiscal theory make sense?

There is a fundamental core of truth in the fiscal theory to the extent that fiscal considerations may dominate monetary policy under certain conditions and have frequently done so in history. In fact, suspension of convertibility to gold or another commodity standard is nothing other than a manifestation of fiscal dominance. Indeed, many episodes of high inflation in the past have been associated with high public debt, for example in several European countries after World War II. When central banks are worried about public debt they are right:

sooner or later high debt may impinge on central bank independence and force their hand.

The precise mechanism described in the fiscal theory of the price level, however, is much more disputed. It is worth mentioning three types of criticism, in particular.

First, say critics such as Willem Buiter of Citigroup, the intertemporal budget constraint of the government is an accounting identity, not an equation describing actual behaviour. It is therefore empty to derive behavioural assumptions from that equation, as the fiscal theory does.

Second, there is an important third way between monetising debt through inflation and raising taxes, which is default on debt – namely, the sovereign does not pay back all its liabilities to bondholders, domestic or foreign or both. A government default is certainly a costly process, but is far from impossible, and history is indeed replete with examples of sovereign debt default and restructuring. Default breaks fiscal dominance and is generally favourable to monetary dominance.[13] For this reason, allowing for sovereign debt is a possible second best for a central bank who wants to maintain monetary dominance. The first best, of course, is to ensure fiscal sustainability and maintain public debt at low levels.

Third, what is relevant is the political economy of the balance of powers between the government and the central bank. Fiscal dominance does not arise all the time, but it is the result of specific factors. With low central bank independence, there may be a tight link between the government fiscal situation and inflation, but this is a different question, namely a question about the quality of institutions in a country. As pointed out for example by Adam Posen, often the relative power of the central bank versus the government depends on personalities and other imponderable factors; in some countries with relatively underdeveloped or mismanaged institutions the central bank is often a voice of reason and competence which may give it influence well beyond its formal powers; Italy is arguably a case in point, with its Governors often taking leading roles in other institutions including serving as prime ministers and Heads of State.

Chris Sims at Princeton University has proposed an interesting perspective on the relative desirability of monetary and fiscal dominance, even though only as a framework for conceptualising the problem rather than a practical guide of actual policy.[14] Assume as given that public debt is high and fiscal sustainability is at risk. As we have seen, there are three options available: (i) increase taxes (or, less likely, cut public spending); (ii) push the central bank to monetise government debt via inflation; (iii) default.[15] Each of these options is unpalatable in its own right. High and variable inflation creates distortions due to sticky prices and monopolistic competition; high taxes are distortionary; and default has high fixed costs, which depend on a host of factors, for example legal provisions in government bonds. The optimal combination of the three options is the path that minimises the overall sum of distortions, and may well involve a combination of all three elements.[16] More likely, however, the chosen path will be that most likely to ensure re-election for incumbent governments. Political economy factors are bound to trump economic logic in determining the way out of high public debt.

Monetary policy in reality: the corridor system

Let us now turn to a second key question surrounding the mainstream approach, which is its description of the practical implementation of policy. Of course, it is not necessary for the model to be precise and detailed about implementation, and it is sufficient that it gives the right insight in terms of the channels whereby monetary policy steers the economy. However, the distance between the allegory of the model and the reality of monetary policy implementation is wide and may be quite misleading. Incidentally, this is one of the reasons why working in a central bank may be helpful – one gains exposure to the practical side.

In the mainstream model, at least in its caricature that I have offered in the previous chapter, monetary policy works by transferring cash to households, who adjust the interest rate depending on how satiated they are with their cash balances.[17] Movements in the interest rate then set in motion the transmission mechanism via the Euler equation and the Phillips curve that we saw in the previous chapter. Note that it is not essential that the money injection is really a transfer: even a swap between central bank money and government bonds has an effect on the nominal interest rate if the former is seen to deliver some type of transaction services that are valued and that bonds cannot provide.

In the reality of today's monetary policy, cash injections to households simply do not exist. Currency in circulation, i.e. the jargon word for cash held by households, is largely interest inelastic (simple introspection should prove this point easily) and must be provided by the banks to customers on demand, and hence by the central bank to the banks also on demand. Imagine if you could not withdraw cash from the cash dispenser because of a monetary policy decision! Moreover, there is practically no direct transaction between the central bank and the public at large, at least in developed countries. In particular, households cannot borrow from the central bank; only banks can. Why this is the case – and it is in principle not obvious that it should be – will be clear in a moment.

Monetary policy works entirely through the cash holdings by banks, i.e. bank reserves. But also here the idea of a well-defined money demand function by banks is misleading. Banks essentially want to hold cash only for two reasons. First, because they are compelled to do so by the central bank due to the reserve requirement (i.e. the requirement to hold a certain percentage of their liabilities as reserves). In normal times they do not require any more reserves than that, and their demand function is therefore a very non-linear (and artificial) one. Second, in a crisis banks may want to hoard central bank money because they lose access to other forms of short-term financing (more on this in Chapter 5). Money demand by banks may well be much larger than normal in a crisis, but is equally not well behaved as in normal times. If the central bank had to base its interest rate control on this fickle money demand function, we would be in for a lot of problems, but fortunately there is no need to do that. What most central banks do is simply to set a corridor for the level of the interest rates. Normally there is a rate at the bottom of the corridor where the banks can deposit money *at* the central bank, and a rate at the top where banks can refinance themselves *from* the central bank.

The supply of central bank money through monetary policy operations at most determines the position of short-term interbank interest rates (say, the overnight interest rate) within the corridor, and not at all the level of the corridor. Monetary policy operations still serve some purpose because banks need to be provided the necessary amount of central bank money to cover the cash withdrawals by their customers and keep the required reserves, but as far as monetary policy is concerned they are *de facto* immaterial. It is certainly possible to argue that what ultimately gives central banks the power to credibly set this corridor is their role as provider of means of payment of last resort, but it is still a far cry from the description typically found in textbooks. In fact, as we will see in Chapter 6, most economists think that central bank interest rate control does not depend at all on the monopoly of the production of paper currency.

Interestingly, the US Federal Reserve – probably the world's most important central bank – has been among the last to join the club of the potential corridor-setters, as it acquired the capability to pay positive interest on reserves in 2008 (although it has not used this capability to this effect during the crisis, when the interest on reserves rather provided a floor for the federal funds rate). This has allowed the Federal Reserve to de-couple policies that influence the size of its balance sheet and hence the amount of reserves (on the liabilities side of its balance sheet) and the stance of monetary policy measured by the short-term interbank interest rate. This change has been helpful, but it also further confirms the notion that it is not necessary to manipulate the amount of bank reserves in order to set the nominal interest rate. A further benefit of the ability to pay interest on reserves is the prospect of banks holding a larger amount of reserves, which are liquid and safe assets and contribute positively to their soundness and stability (see Chapter 5).

Another compelling deviation of reality from the textbook description is the role of collateral. Monetary policy operations are not really carried out by transferring central bank money on the banks' accounts, but by lending to banks against collateral which often, but not necessarily, takes the form of government bonds. The fundamental reason why monetary policy is implemented in this way is that central banks, as agents of public policy accountable to the parliament, must protect their balance sheet and prevent borrowers from abusing the system and stealing public money. The cleanest way to be sure to be paid back would be to swap central bank money with other assets, taking into account market prices, but this has a host of consequences for banks' balance sheet and it is fraught with significant costs (say, settlement and clearing) especially if carried out at high frequency. A simpler method to ensure the integrity of the central bank balance sheet is to lend against good collateral, so that the assets used as collateral never leave the balance sheet of the borrower.

The following example helps to clarify the intuition. Suppose that I need to borrow a significant amount of money to finance a project. It may be more efficient to use my house as collateral rather than selling it, undertaking the project, and then purchasing it back if the project is successful. The transactions costs are just much more contained if I pledge my house and it never leaves my ownership.

There are two important consequences stemming from the fact that monetary policy is implemented in this way. First, the system is based on a highly developed system for managing collateral which requires having sophisticated and well-staffed institutions as counterparties. This prevents central banks from doing business with the public at large, as it is inconceivable that a sophisticated and largely automatised collateral management could be built for them. This has the sometimes not very palatable consequence that only banks can borrow at comparatively low rates from central banks, while ordinary citizens cannot. Second, collateral management is a very important part of monetary policy, which is a fact that is almost always completely forgotten in textbooks as well as overlooked by observers of monetary policy. What assets are accepted, and what haircut is applied to risky assets, are material elements of monetary policy, sometimes more important than setting the level of the interest rate. (The haircut is the reduction in the value of the asset pledged as collateral compared with its nominal value. For example, a bond nominally worth 100 euro may be valued at 50 because it is risky, which implies a haircut of 50%.) Collateral policy is especially relevant in crisis times, as we will see in Chapter 5.

The natural rate hypothesis

Let us now move to the third implicit assumption of the mainstream model that is not really innocent at all, namely the 'natural rate' assumption.

In December 1967, a short and energetic man took the podium as President of the American Economic Association. His address is considered to have been a landmark of the so-called natural rate hypothesis.[18] In his own words,

> The 'natural rate of unemployment,' in other words, is the level that would be ground out by the Walrasian system of general equilibrium equations, provided there is imbedded in them the actual structural characteristics of the labor and commodity markets, including market imperfections, stochastic variability in demands and supplies, the cost of gathering information about job vacancies and labor availabilities, the costs of mobility, and so on.

That man is, of course, Milton Friedman, a very influential thinker of monetary policy whom we will see again in the course of this book. Mainstream monetary policy would be unthinkable without his influence, and the convergence to the 'natural' level of variables is the Holy Grail of any central banker with at least some degree of belief in the mainstream New Keynesian model. Let us recall that the New Keynesian mainstream is ultimately built on a Real Business Cycle model where households and firms are rational, they have no money illusion (hence only real quantities matter), and money is neutral.

Thus, according to the natural rate hypothesis, real variables are determined independently of nominal variables, at least in the long term. Money is neutral, and supply and demand are disconnected; short-term fluctuations in demand (such as those created by monetary policy under sticky prices) do not matter for the economy's productive capacity in the long term. Moreover, there is a valid reason for business cycle fluctuations that are not connected to monetary factors; these may be shifts in taste (say, how patient consumers are) or technology (say, a new IT product is introduced successfully). The 'natural' level of macro variables pins down the level that would prevail in the absence of nominal distortions such as sticky prices, and which reflect the fundamental factors just mentioned. In modern New Keynesian models, unknown to Milton Friedman at the time, this corresponds to the flexible price equilibrium.

But does the natural rate hypothesis stand close scrutiny? What is a possible test of the natural rate hypothesis? One could engineer a pure demand shock, for example by running an expansionary monetary policy. If one could also measure the economy's supply side or productive capacity without error, then it would be possible to trace the effect of the initial shock and test for the natural rate hypothesis. Unfortunately for economists, it is not possible to run controlled experiments in macroeconomics, and we need to leave them to the happier lot of physicists and other 'hard' scientists. Moreover, it is not possible to measure the productive capacity of an economy without error, and moreover it is very likely to depend itself on actual macroeconomic developments. Therefore, a direct empirical test of the natural rate hypothesis is difficult and I know of no conclusive one. We simply don't know for sure if Milton Friedman and his followers are right.

However, what we can do is to speculate on the possible mechanisms whereby the natural rate hypothesis can fail, and ask ourselves whether these mechanisms are plausible and important enough to play a material role. There are at least three of them to consider.[19]

Hysteresis

'Hysteresis' is the dependence of the state of a system on its history, and comes from the Greek word ὑστέρησις which signals a 'coming short' or 'deficiency'. A real life example of hysteresis is when, for example, you push an object on a downhill path, and it continues to roll down well beyond the effect of the initial push. Hysteresis, generally speaking, breaks down the natural rate hypothesis. An important and plausible form of hysteresis is in unemployment. If I lose my job, after a while my skills decline. I become not only less good at my work, but also less employable in other jobs.[20] The problem is larger, the longer the time in unemployment. Many equilibrium models see unemployment as a sort of holiday, deliberately chosen by agents,[21] but in reality unemployment is often traumatic and accompanied by a significant loss of welfare and human capital. According to research, this is particularly true for men and it is one of the few life events for which there is no recovery in terms of happiness or life satisfaction, more so even than the death of a relative, for example.[22] There is every reason to think that unemployment hysteresis is important. If a temporary demand shock increases unemployment, it may make the unemployed less marketable, increasing the natural rate of unemployment. Hence this is a first plausible deviation from the natural rate hypothesis. According to recent research, unemployment hysteresis can lead to multiple equilibria; the economy shifts without apparent reason between high and low employment states.

Investment

A second possibility for a violation of the natural rate hypothesis is investment, i.e. the build-up over time of the capital stock – for example, machinery used in factories, office buildings, or infrastructure such as highways or airports, as well as intangible capital such as education and organisational skills. Because investment is the *change* in the capital stock (after correcting for capital depreciation), a boost to investment has a lasting impact on the economy's productive capacity (think of that as a combination of capital and labour). In fact, the effects of monetary policy shocks are more persistent in models with investment. However, as long as capital has a positive depreciation rate (so it loses some value over time, as machines get rusty, buildings become decrepit, and so forth) the effects are not permanent, so this is strictly speaking a violation of the natural rate hypothesis if we speak about the very long term.

The death of valuable firms

Third and final, demand conditions can clearly influence the birth and death of firms. By itself, the death of a firm is an event with no macroeconomic consequence, and birth and death rates may even be positively correlated; for example, the death rate of banks is very low, and their birth rate is also (perhaps worryingly) low. However, the concern is that abrupt shifts in demand, even if temporary, can 'break the back' of otherwise valuable firms, which may lead to the loss of valuable human and organisational capital and hence impinge on the economy's productive capacity. This argument is also sometimes made for entire industrial districts, such as the automobile industry in Detroit or the Italian North East. In other cases, the firm in question has systemic relevance for the whole economy. This is an argument that governments often use to prop up 'strategic' firms – an argument however that can be easily abused and has always to be taken with a grain of salt.

Optimal monetary policy under hysteresis

If hysteresis induced by any of these factors is quantitatively important, what is the consequence for monetary policy? How does it matter that the natural rate hypothesis breaks down? There are two important elements to consider. First, temporary fluctuations in demand are more important and their effect more persistent than otherwise, so it makes sense for monetary policy to put a larger weight on output stabilisation, and allow a moderately higher variability in the inflation rate. On the other hand, monetary policy actions by themselves have a more lasting impact, so the monetary policy instrument may have to be used more parsimoniously for given objectives. In practice, this implies moving the interest rate less in order to achieve more (output) stabilisation. This is an area where interesting research is being done and more should be coming in the near future.[23]

Notes

1 A fourth one will arise after the treatment of the zero lower bound problem, which we will see in Chapter 4.
2 Cargill, T. and G. P. O'Driscoll, 'Federal Reserve Independence: Reality or Myth?', *The Cato Journal* 33, 2013, 417–435; for a book treatment see S. Binder and M. Spindel, *The Myth of Independence: How Congress Governs the Federal Reserve*, Princeton: Princeton University Press, 2017.
3 Barro, R. and D. Gordon, 'Rules, Discretion and Reputation in a Model of Monetary Policy', *Journal of Monetary Economics* 12, 1, 1983, 101–121.
4 Rogoff, K., 'The Optimal Commitment to an Intermediate Target', *Quarterly Journal of Economics* 100, 1985, 1169–1190.
5 Posen, A., 'Why Central Bank Independence does not Cause Low Inflation: There is no Institutional Fix for Politics', in O'Brien, R. (Ed.), *Finance and the International Economy*, Oxford: Oxford University Press, pp. 41–66.
6 See Campillo, M. and J. Miron, 'Why Does Inflation Differ across Countries?', in *Reducing Inflation: Motivation and Strategy*, National Bureau of Economic Research, pp. 335–362. For a critical assessment of this view see Brumm, H., 'Inflation and Central Bank Independence: Conventional Wisdom Redux', *Journal of Money, Credit and Banking* 32, 4, 2000, 807–19.
7 See Sargent, T. and N. Wallace, 'Some Unpleasant Monetarist Arithmetic', *Quarterly Review* 5, 3, 1981.
8 Leeper, E., 'Equilibria under "Active" and "Passive" Monetary and Fiscal Policies', *Journal of Monetary Economics* 27, 1, 1991, 129–147.
9 Technically, if the central bank follows the Taylor principle, inflation is actually overdeterminate rather than indeterminate, because there are two equations setting the inflation rate and they disagree. Thanks to John Cochrane for pointing this out (private correspondence).
10 Rockoff, H., 'War, Money, and Inflation in the United States from the Revolution to the Vietnam War', 2014, mimeo.
11 Rockoff (op. cit.) points to an interesting difference between in the US experience between WWI and WWII: in WWI the Fed lent to banks using government bonds as collateral, in WWII it bought bonds directly, but the end results were practically the same. We will come back to this question in more general terms in the next chapter.
12 Rockoff (op. cit.)
13 Uribe, M., 'A Fiscal Theory of Sovereign Risk', *Journal of Monetary Economics* 53, 8, 2006, 1857–1875.
14 Sims, C., 'Paper Money', *American Economic Review* 103, 2, 2013, 563–84.
15 I am assuming here that it is not possible to liquidate public sector assets, which is sometimes also a viable way to reduce public debt.
16 A model based analysis of this choice is contained in de Resende and Rebei (2008) where the parameter driving the relative weight of monetary and fiscal dominance can be determined exogenously. They show that a higher degree of fiscal dominance does lead to higher trend inflation, but also that full central bank independence and monetary dominance are not necessarily welfare optimal in all cases. See de Resende, C. and N. Rebei, 'The Welfare Implications of Fiscal Dominance', Bank of Canada Staff Working Papers, 2008.
17 Note that in this book I am using the word 'cash' as a strict synonym for banknotes or whatever very close substitute for them, e.g. coins. I am not referring to the loose use of

'cash' as a synonym for short-term assets often encountered in the corporate finance and management literature, which I find imprecise.

18 Friedman, M., 'The Role of Monetary Policy', *American Economic Review*, 58, 1, 1968, 1–17.
19 Reifschneider, D., W. Wascher, and D. Wilcox, 'Aggregate Supply in the United States: Recent Developments and Implications for the Conduct of Monetary Policy', *IMF Economic Review* 63, 1, 2015, 71–109.
20 Blanchard, O. J. and L. H. Summers, 'Hysteresis in Unemployment', *European Economic Review* 31, 1–2, 1987, 288–295.
21 Hence the Great Recession has been dubbed as the 'Great Vacation'.
22 Clark, A. E. and A. J. Oswald, 'Unhappiness and Unemployment', *Economic Journal*, 104, 424, 1994, 648–659.
23 For example, Kienzler and Schmid (2013) argue that more hysteresis implies more weight on output stabilisation (e.g. as in the US Federal Reserve 'dual mandate'). See Kienzler, D. and K. D. Schmid, 'Monetary Policy and Hysteresis in Potential Output', IMK Working Paper 116, 2013.

4
THE ZERO LOWER BOUND PROBLEM

If you get a banknote out of your wallet, it looks innocent enough. But your banknote can be a weapon of mass destruction for the global economy. At the end of this chapter, you may not look at your banknote in the same way.

Paper banknotes have many desirable features, for example portability, and there is a reason behind their worldwide success as a means of payment. In Chapter 6 we will briefly look into the history of the creation and diffusion of paper currency. But there is an undesirable characteristic of paper currency that makes it highly problematic from the point of view of monetary policy: it is difficult to write an interest rate on banknotes, because they are a 'bearer bond' that gives a right to the holder independent of his or her identity. Therefore, banknotes have a zero interest rate.

Because there is a safe asset, issued by the government, with nominal interest rate at zero, it can be concluded that no other short-term asset can carry a nominal interest rate below zero. This is commonly known as the 'zero bound' on the interest rate, and it creates an important complication to monetary policy making. Note that the zero bound is not exactly at zero. Because paper currency has significant storage costs (it is not risk free to store cash in the proverbial mattress), the nominal interest rate can in fact be a bit below zero. Nobody knows exactly how much, but probably somewhere between minus half a percentage point and one percentage point per year is the effective zero bound. What is crucial from an analytical point of view is that there is an effective bound, it does not really matter all that much whether the bound is *exactly* at zero.

Clearly, the *real* interest rate *can* be negative, and that is also true of the Friedmanian natural real interest rate, reflecting the economy's fundamentals. (Again, the real interest rate is the difference between the nominal interest rate and expected inflation.) If I expect to be poor tomorrow, I will want to save money to smooth consumption over time. If everybody is in the same situation, this will result in a negative real interest rate in equilibrium, due to the excess of saving over investment. If inflation is low and stable, a strongly negative equilibrium real interest rate should lead, in principle, to a negative *nominal* interest rate. But this is precisely where the nominal interest rate cannot go because of the existence of paper currency. All this creates a 'silly asymmetry' in monetary policy making. The interest rate can be raised by the central bank to whatever value can be appropriate, but it cannot be lowered below zero even if the economic situation requires it.

An economy under a zero bound has a quaint behaviour in several respects, and we are going to see some of it in this chapter. In general this is still an important unresolved aspect of modern monetary policy making which has significant macroeconomic consequences. Given this importance, I am always quite surprised to see how little the general public seems to know about the problem. Although I know of no direct evidence, it is quite safe to conclude that most people are mostly completely unaware of the zero bound problem. A main reason is that this discussion is never reported in the media.

A Gesell tax?

In theory, charging an interest on paper currency should not be impossible. For example, one could print a date of issuance on each banknote and define an increasing or decreasing value over time. A banknote could be worth, say, 50 euro at issuance, and increase in value by 1% every year, so that, for example, a banknote issued in 2010 would be worth approximately 55 euro in 2020. However, an unfortunate consequence of a banknote carrying an interest is that it does not exchange at par with another banknote, and with goods and services. That feature, in turn, would seriously undermine its role in facilitating transactions, which derives to a large extent from having a fixed nominal value. As a result, practically the world over paper currency has a nominal rate of return of exactly zero.[1]

One way to implement a nominal negative interest rate on paper currency would be to tax it despite the fact that it is a bearer bond, by some use of a stamp or expiry date. This idea is typically associated with the name of Silvio Gesell, an anarchist who was among the first to popularise the idea that money should be taxed in order to prevent the formation of rents and the creation of a class of rentiers. Other authors have proposed the idea of a time-varying interest rate on currency which is activated only when the zero lower bound (ZLB) is a problem and not otherwise. It is even possible to build models where taxing currency is optimal in itself, because it leads to an increase in the velocity in circulation of money and to more transactions being carried out, by preventing hoarding – one may want money that 'burns' in the pocket.[2]

But would people want to hold a banknote at all – and use it as a means of payment – if they know that it is going to depreciate over time? In other words, money might lose one of its main functions, being a store of value. This is not necessarily a problem in itself unless the expected depreciation is very large or fast – indeed banknote holders would have nowhere else to go if the nominal interest rate were negative on all short-term assets, such as Treasury bills. In other words, even paper currency with a negative rate would be a good store of value, *relatively speaking*.

The main reason why a Gesell tax has almost never been applied has to do mainly with reasons of practical convenience than anything else. It is just less practical to use banknotes if they also have an expiry date or if different banknotes have different values – the main advantage of banknotes is to minimise transaction costs, and they cannot accomplish their goal if using them is costly or time consuming.

Why didn't we see it coming?

One way to illustrate the problem of the zero bound is to think in terms of a simple Taylor rule whereby a central bank adjusts the nominal short-term interest rate to inflation developments, with elasticity higher than one. In the presence of very low or negative inflation, for example in a recession, this rule may occasionally call for a negative interest rate, precisely what is impossible under the zero bound.

Up to a decade ago and lulled by the Great Moderation, policy-makers and economists thought that only the Japanese would have to face this problem, and it was unlikely that any other advanced country would encounter it. For example, the European Central Bank (ECB), in its 2003 review of the monetary policy strategy, revealed that:

> In order to calibrate the adequate safety margin for inflation rates in this respect, we took into account the studies which have tried to assess the likelihood of nominal interest rates hitting the zero lower bound for various levels of inflation objectives. Results in this area differ to some extent, as they depend on a number of specific assumptions. But the available studies indicate that the likelihood decreases to very low levels when the central bank aims at an inflation rate above 1%. *We are thus convinced that focusing on inflation of below but close to 2% provides a sufficient safety margin against nominal interest rates hitting the zero lower bound.*[3] [emphasis added]

I don't want to single out the ECB – which happens to be my employer – here, the complacent view was really a widespread one.

This implies that with an inflation target of 2% (a typical value for inflation targeting central banks) the prospect of hitting the zero bound is remote. This was the view prevailing in the central bank community up to the mid-2000s, before the global financial crisis hit.

Why was the zero bound considered to be confined to Japan and not to be a problem for other countries? The narrative at the time was that Japan had been hit by an unusual crash in real estate values and lending after the boom in the 1980s, and also by an unusual slowdown of potential output growth in the 1990s, partly due to its fast population ageing. Dozens of articles have been written on the

Japanese experience, but very few of them sounded an alarm bell for other advanced countries. Europe and the US continued to enjoy solidly positive nominal interest rates up to the global financial crisis, so the prospect of hitting the zero bound was seen as remote. Now, of course, almost the entire group of advanced countries has either hit the zero bound or is still there, notably in Europe (and obviously Japan).

Partly because of this lack of imagination, there wasn't and in part there still isn't a clear consensus of what happens when the economy hits the zero bound. In its most basic incarnation the New Keynesian model would imply that inflation becomes indeterminate or stuck at very low levels. Recall that, according to the mainstream model that we described in Chapter 2, the determinacy of inflation depends on the central bank following the Taylor principle. If the central bank is prevented from adjusting the interest rate in the manner foreseen in the Taylor principle, inflation becomes indeterminate. The zero lower bound breaks the Taylor principle in a region of the interest rate rule, and hence, in principle, it must also make inflation indeterminate, as long as the ZLB is binding.

Interestingly, this is not what seems to have happened in Japan, which has been at the zero bound almost continuously since the early 1990s. Rather than bouncing around or becoming indeterminate, inflation has been stuck at very low or mildly negative levels. This is only apparently in contrast with the mainstream model, as we will now see.

The peril with Taylor rules

A less common way to look at the role of the zero bound is the 'second steady state' described in a (until recently not very widely known) 2001 article by Jess Benhabib at New York University and Stephanie Schmitt-Grohe and Marin Uribe at Columbia University, 'The Perils of Taylor Rules'.[4] In general, the 'steady state' of the model is the solution prevailing in the long term, when all transitory shocks have run their course. For example, the steady state of a pendulum is its situation at rest, to which it returns after a gentle push makes it swing for some time (a less gentle push might destabilize it and move to another steady state).

The authors note that the Taylor principle has a point of failure if interest rates are bound at zero. In that case, there is not only one (non-explosive) steady state but *two*: the second steady state is characterised by interest rates at the zero bound and inflation persistently negative, but not spiralling out of control. Call this the Japanese steady state.

It is in fact a quite robust prediction, as it applies to a variety of different models. The unintended steady state has a strong 'Neo-Fisherian' taste because it can be described using the Fisher equation, according to which the nominal interest rate is the sum of the real interest rate and expected inflation. If the real interest rate is fixed in the long term and pinned down by real factors outside the control of the central bank, then a low interest rate is only compatible with low inflation over time.

The world appears lopsided at the unintended steady state. Reducing interest rates is counter-productive. Actually, it can be shown that a policy rule that promises not to lower interest rates below a certain level (say 1.5%) prevents the unintended steady state.[5] The key is not to encourage a permanently low interest rate outcome.

We cannot say for sure if Japan, or indeed other advanced countries, are in this 'permazero'[6] state – and indeed the fact that interest rates are rising above zero at least in the United States appears to contradict this idea. However, it is important to recognise that we don't really know if and how monetary policy works if we are in the vicinity of the zero bound. My view is that the low interest rates, low inflation second steady state is something we should take quite seriously and is not only a theoretical curiosum. Much of its plausibility depends on whether we can get into the unintended steady state in a way that is realistic in terms of the way people form expectations, on which we still don't know enough.[7]

ZLB quaintness

The second steady state is only one manifestation of the many strange things that can happen when the economy hits the zero bound, a bit like the law of physics in a black hole.[8] One of them is the so-called 'paradox of toil': positive supply shocks, say due to technological innovation, can actually be contractionary in the short term.[9] Normally, a positive supply shock raises potential output and lowers inflation temporarily: this is in fact a defining characteristic of supply shocks – consumers benefit from cheaper and more abundant goods. Under the zero bound, however, the fall in inflation leads to a rise in the *ex ante* real interest rate, through the Fisher equation (see Chapter 2). In turn, the (unwanted) rise in the real interest rate encourages consumers to save, and prevents firms from investing. The result can be, paradoxically, a recession. Under the ZLB, productivity enhancements can become a very Sisyphean task!

A general feature in the reaction of the economy to shocks under the ZLB is that the effects of demand shocks are amplified, whereas the effects of supply shocks are dampened. The reason is that positive demand shocks imply a rise in both income and inflation, and the latter has a further expansionary effect (acting through the Fisher equation and the Euler equation that we saw in the last chapter) especially at the ZLB when interest rates are at zero and do not increase, unless the shock is very strong. In normal times, a demand shock also leads to a rise in the interest rate, which dampens the propagation of the initial shock.

Another implication of the zero bound is in the balance of activism between monetary and fiscal policy. As noted, the mainstream model foresees that the primary tool to smooth the business cycle is monetary policy, and fiscal policy should be rather passive and focus on long-term goals and maintain fiscal sustainability. Under the zero bound, this principle reverses. Because monetary policy is constrained, fiscal policy should share more of the burden of stabilising the business cycle. At the same time, the effects of fiscal expansion (the fiscal multipliers) may be stronger under the zero bound, because when the interest rate is stuck at zero it will not rise after, say, a rise in government spending, therefore not 'crowding out' investment as it normally does outside of a zero bound situation. ('Crowding out' means that higher government spending raises aggregate demand and inflation, leading to higher interest rates; these in turn discourage private investment, which loses out to public investment and spending.)

Although fiscal policy becomes more effective and important at the ZLB, it is not necessarily available in the way that would be necessary. Public debt may be already high and government sustainability stretched, which may in turn make fiscal expansions less effective.[10] Moreover, central banks are ultimately responsible for the management of aggregate demand in the economy, and cannot think of always being 'bailed out' at the ZLB by the fiscal authority. Therefore, central banks have to find their own way out of the ZLB.

Five ways out of the ZLB

By now it should be clear that the zero bound is a significant problem for monetary policy. What a monetary policy would want to do is to run a policy that overcomes the zero bound, i.e. set aggregate demand at a level that would result from a negative interest rate, even if that cannot be obtained. The common idea is to set policy so that its effects are the same as those which would prevail if the nominal short-term interest rate would be allowed to be negative. In fact, the effectiveness of these measures is often gauged by some kind of 'shadow' interest rate, i.e. the interest rate below zero that truly corresponds to the current stance of policy and that the zero-bounded interest rate cannot properly measure. Figure 4.1 reports one of such measures for the United States, and at the same time illustrates just how widespread the ZLB problem is in advanced countries.

In the rest of this chapter, we are going to see four of five possible ways to circumvent the zero bound. It is important to note from the outset that none of them is still a fool-proof way to overcome the ZLB. Economists are divided on whether any of these method are really effective, and it is fair to say that the profession is still rather divided on whether there is any practical solution at all for the ZLB problem.

The five remedies that we will see are (i) increasing the inflation target; (ii) lowering long-term interest rates, rather than the short-term interest rate, i.e. reducing term and risk premia; (iii) abolishing paper currency; (iv) price level targeting; and (v) de-linking the unit of account from the medium of exchange. Because the third remedy is the main subject of Chapter 6, I will not go into details in this chapter, and I will concentrate on the other four, in particular the second.

It is also useful to clarify that I will consider a situation where the zero bound is a general problem and not limited to one country. I will therefore not consider the depreciation of the exchange rate as the main channel to get out of the zero bound, as was proposed some time ago for example by Lars Svensson at the Stockholm School of Economics in his 'fool-proof' way.[11]

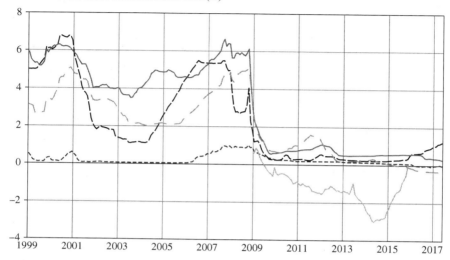

FIGURE 4.1 Short-term interest rates in the world's major industrialised economies. The Wu-Xia 'shadow' federal funds rate is an indicator of the interest rate that takes into account the effect of non-standard measures such as QE.

A higher inflation target?

It is not difficult to see that low inflation breeds the risk of hitting the zero bound. Due to the Fisher equation, the nominal interest rate is the sum of the real interest rate and expected inflation. In the steady state, the nominal interest rate is the sum of the equilibrium real interest rate (think of an exogenous parameter driven by preferences and technology) and the inflation target. Therefore a low inflation target reduces the steady state value of the nominal interest rate. Suppose the equilibrium real rate is 1% per year, and the inflation target is 2% per year, one would expect a long-term average of the nominal interest rate to be 3%. If the inflation target were raised to 4%, the steady state level would become 1% + 4% = 5%. Given the same variability of the business cycle, which drives the interest rate away from its steady state level, it is much easier to hit zero if interest rates average around 3% than when they average 5%. At the same time, we know that the welfare cost of inflation kicks in only at a higher level of inflation; there is probably really not much difference between 2% and 4% as far as the welfare of citizens is concerned, as we have seen.[12] Therefore, a possible remedy to the zero bound would be for central banks to increase the inflation target to, say, 4%. This is indeed the main idea behind a 2010 paper by a team of IMF economists, Olivier

Blanchard, Giovanni Dell'Ariccia and Paolo Mauro, and re-iterated with additional arguments by others such as Laurence Ball.[13]

There is a certain logic and simplicity (in a positive sense) behind this proposal, but central banks have generally not been impressed, so that the proposal has not, to my knowledge, been seriously discussed in central banking circles, although central bankers have become somewhat less negative to the idea over time. Their criticism is threefold. First, inflation targets should not be changed too frequently. There is a value in anchoring agents' expectations around a particular value, and central banks prize the hard-won credibility of their 2% inflation targets. A variant of this criticism is the 'slippery slope' argument: if we change the inflation target once, why not twice, then thrice, and so on until inflation is completely out of control. Second, there are important transition questions, in particular in a situation where central banks struggle to even achieve their lower inflation targets. The impossibility of reaching a 2%, let alone a 4%, inflation target could taint the whole idea and harm the credibility of central banks. In theory at least, a higher inflation target gives central banks an additional impact on the economy, via the Euler equation (recall, the equation linking today's consumption to tomorrow's expected consumption and the real interest rate). Say that the short-term interest rate is at the zero bound; a higher expectation for inflation following a higher inflation target reduces the *ex ante* real interest rate, with expansionary effects. But this presupposes that the change in the inflation target is credible, which it may not be in the current circumstances. Third, and perhaps most fundamentally, central banks are convinced that their non-standard measures are effective in overcoming the zero bound and reaching their inflation target through monetary policy alone. As we will soon see, whether these non-standard measures are really effective is open to debate.

Price level targeting

An alternative monetary policy strategy containing some of the positive elements of a higher inflation target, but operating with a different mechanism, is price level targeting.[14]

Before discussing price level targeting, it should be recalled that the mainstream inflation targeting approach has the little-known feature that past deviations of inflation from the target are *not* subsequently compensated for. If my inflation target is 2% and this year inflation turns out to be 1%, I will not compensate by targeting 3% inflation next year. The central bank will rather stick to the 2% target. Doing so, it is presumed, lends even more credibility and predictability to the inflation target, and it is easier to understand for a general public who has other things to think about and values simplicity. Therefore, under inflation targeting 'bygones are bygones': inflation misses from the past do not matter for current policy (In my experience most non-economists, when confronted with this feature of inflation targeting, tend to look puzzled).

Under price level targeting, this is not the case: missing inflation on the downside implies targeting a miss to the upside in the future, so as to keep the price level on a predetermined path. It is a common misunderstanding that price level targeting implies absolute stability of the price level; it is compatible with a mildly rising price level, for example. The key difference with inflation targeting is really the practice of compensating for past misses.

An advantage of price level targeting over inflation targeting is a higher predictability of the price level at long horizons. This can be easily quantified. Suppose that under price level targeting the price level is expected to increase by 2% per year; after 20 years, it can be expected to be about 50% higher than now, obtained by compounding 2% every year. Now suppose that inflation can be 2% on average, but with random deviations by 1% every year that are not compensated for in subsequent years. In this regime one can expect the price level to be between about 37% and 63% 20 years out with a confidence level of 95 per cent, which may be a material source of uncertainty in a long-term contract.

Another advantage of price level targeting is that, if it is credible (a big if), it works so as to facilitate monetary policy in particular under the zero bound. Expectations under price level targeting work counter-cyclically: suppose we have low inflation due to recession, and inflation is under-shooting the target. Agents correctly expect the central bank to aim at higher inflation in the future. For given short-term and long-term interest rates, this implies a lower *ex ante* real interest rate (again, via the Fisher equation), which is expansionary. Because an expansion of activity leads to higher inflation, higher inflation expectations are validated and the economy may escape from the zero bound, under the right conditions, in a way that would be impossible under inflation targeting.

If price level targeting has these two key advantages over inflation targeting (higher predictability of the price level and escaping the zero bound), why haven't central banks adopted it already? Not so fast.

In fact, there is only one historical example of price level targeting, namely, Sweden between 1931 and 1937. Sweden had abandoned the Gold Standard in the fall of 1931, and decided to target the price level in a move that can be seen as an early adoption of something similar to what later has become known as inflation targeting.[15] An intellectual father of this decision was Knut Wicksell, a Swedish economist who later became known for his work on the natural rate of interest, which is sometimes called the 'Wicksellian' rate after him. Why did price level targeting eventually end in Sweden? In part, because the strategy of price level targeting was not meant to be a permanent abandonment of the Gold Standard. But more fundamentally, stable prices were not considered to be sufficient for Sweden to get out of the depression – price level targeting was just seen as a useful element in terms of preventing deflation, with a strong element of fiscal and monetary cooperation.

All in all, therefore, price level targeting has not been a very popular strategy so far. One key reason is that price level targeting is *fragile* as an optimal monetary policy strategy. It works very well if the conditions are ideal, but badly if they are not. In particular, one element of fragility is in the expectations formation strategy. If expectations are even only partly backward looking or the price level target is not fully credible, outcomes can actually be worse than under inflation targeting. Suppose, again, that we are in recession and with low inflation, with short-term interest rates stuck at the zero bound. Price level targeting requires not only to bring inflation back to target but to even over-shoot the target. If agents form expectations based on past inflation, it will be a very tall order for the central bank to achieve an inflation rate higher than the target, almost a recipe for failure. In turn, repeated failure by the central bank sets the stage for loss of credibility and eventually collapse of the strategy.[16]

For all these reasons, price level targeting is not a serious contender for a solution to the zero bound problem, but it is better not to dismiss it right away, because we do not have plenty of good alternatives to build on, as we will soon see.

Non-standard policies

The solution to the ZLB that is favoured by most central banks is to make recourse to so-called non-standard monetary policies. The objective of these policies is to influence financial prices beyond the short-term interest rate which is the mainstream approach (hence the name 'non-standard'). More concretely, the objective of these policies is to lower interest rates at long maturity (hence compress the 'term spread', the difference between long- and short-term interest rates) and/or risk premia, i.e. the difference in expected return between risky and safe assets, say the spread between bank lending rates to customers with different riskiness. The idea behind all these policies is the same: it is the attempt to stimulate aggregate demand via the Euler equation (see Chapter 2) by acting on interest rates or expected returns other than the short-term rate, which is constrained by the ZLB. Hence these policies are effective in providing stimulus to aggregate demand and indirectly inflation only to the extent that those interest rates are relevant for aggregate demand in their own right. It is indeed plausible that long-term interest rates and risk premia do matter for demand. For example, it is plausible that household borrowing and hence consumption spending depends on the effective rates that households pay, inclusive of risk premia, rather than on the risk free interest rate at which only (low debt) governments can borrow. Therefore, a policy that is able to influence those rates has a reasonable chance to succeed in providing stimulus at the ZLB, hopefully ultimately allowing the economy to escape from it.

There is more than one way in which non-standard policies can achieve their objective to lower long-term interest rates and risk premia. Usually we make a distinction between policies aimed at lowering long-term risk free interest rates ('forward guidance' and 'quantitative easing') and aimed at lowering risk premia ('credit easing').

Before we consider each of them in turn, there is a general qualification to be made. Even non-standard policies, effective as they may be, cannot be a full solution to the ZLB in all circumstances, as they face diminishing returns. Even long-term interest rates and risk premia are eventually bound at zero, in the same way as short-term interest rates. In Japan at the time of writing, for example, the entire yield curve up to a maturity of 20 years is at the zero lower bound. It is an empirical matter whether central banks can provide enough additional stimulus at the zero bound before they reach these unavoidable limits. This is in particular an important matter to consider if, as seems entirely possible, central banks are bound to hit the ZLB frequently in the future, due to low equilibrium real interest rates and inflation. Sooner or later, some central banks may find out that even the most aggressive non-standard policies are not enough.

Forward guidance

The apparently simplest way for the central bank to influence long-term interest rates could be to tell market participants that it will keep future short-term interest rates at a certain level. As we have seen in Chapter 2, the central bank exerts a good control over short-term interest rates. If long-term interest rates are the expectation of future short-term interest rates (this is called in the jargon 'the expectations theory of the term structure'), then a policy of so-called forward guidance should be effective in guiding long-term rates. The central bank could essentially say, 'I commit to keep short-term interest rates at the zero bound for the next 5 years'; if the central bank is believed by market participants, interest rates at that longer maturity, say 5-year or 10-year, should converge to the level communicated by the central bank.

According to recent research, there are two distinct types of forward guidance: 'Delphic' and 'Odyssean'.[17] The oracle of Delphi forecast the future but promised nothing; Odysseus asked his fellow sailors to bind him to the mast and to keep him bound whatever the sirens would do to entice him. In the less dramatic central banking context, a Delphic forward guidance says, 'I expect to keep interest rates low for a protracted period given current economic circumstances as I see them'. An Odyssean forward guidance says, 'I commit to keep short-term rates at the zero lower bound no matter what', where the 'no matter what' can actually be further specified (conditional forward guidance). For example, conditionality may be qualitative (say, 'until the economy recovers sufficiently') or quantitative (say, 'until the unemployment rate reaches 5%'). One example of the latter is the so-called 'Evans rule' at the US Federal Reserve: in 2012, the central bank communicated that it:

> decided to keep the target range for the federal funds rate at 0 to 1/4 percent and currently anticipates that this exceptionally low range for the federal funds rate will be appropriate at least as long as the unemployment rate remains above 6–1/2 percent, inflation between one and two years ahead is projected to be no more than a half percentage point above the Committee's 2 percent longer-run goal, and longer-term inflation expectations continue to be well anchored.[18]

It is important to note that the transmission channels are different between Delphic and Odyssean forward guidance. In the Delphic guidance, the central bank is steering market expectations by removing a source of uncertainty on the likely future course of policy. Suppose that the market is uncertain if the central bank is likely to behave in a hawkish (leaning to higher interest rates) or dovish (leaning towards lower interest rates) way in the future: by communicating to the market participants that the central bank is currently in a dovish orientation, expectations may be focused on the low interest rate expectation, thereby influencing interest rates at longer maturities. One downside of Delphic forward guidance, however, is that it may reveal that the central bank is pessimistic about the economy looking forward; if households and firms believe that the central bank has superior knowledge of the economy, they might revise their growth expectations downward, which might have a contractionary effect in its own right, despite lower long-term interest rates. Therefore, there is a risk that Delphic guidance is counterproductive.

Odyssean forward guidance is more unambiguously expansionary, but it is still beset by considerable problems. First, this type of forward guidance has to be believed by the market participants. They may have the legitimate suspicion that, when push comes to shove, the central bank will renege on previous commitments and behave in the future in the way that current economic circumstances suggest. Odyssean guidance essentially says, 'I will not raise interest rates in the future even if future circumstances will demand it', because this is crucial for pushing down long-term rates now. But when the future circumstances come and the central bank is out of the ZLB, it is not clear what its incentive could be, especially if in the meanwhile the decision making bodies (say, the chairman) are different. For example, should the current Chair of the Federal Reserve, Jerome H. Powell, acting under President Trump, feel bound in her actions by the forward guidance expressed, say, under Chairman Ben Bernanke, under President Obama?

Conditionality is another aspect that has proven to be problematic, in particular when specified in quantitative terms. Suppose that the central bank says, 'I will maintain interest rates at the ZLB as long as the unemployment rate remains above 5%'. When the time comes that the unemployment rate reaches 5%, the central bank may have reconsidered the importance of that indicator for inflationary pressure. It may have found out, say, that the unemployment rate is a less robust guide to inflationary pressure than it used to be, and may have to renege on previous communication. This bears the risk that, over time, forward guidance is seen as no more than cheap talk; and indeed empirical evidence suggests that forward guidance on its own (i.e., not accompanied by other non-standard policies) is not very effective in steering long-term interest rates in the desired direction.

An interesting puzzle surrounding forward guidance is that, in the typical New Keynesian model, this policy is actually super-powerful, which seems counter-intuitive also given that the empirical evidence on its effectiveness is at best mixed. This hinges on the fact that, again in the most typical mainstream model, the further out forward guidance, the bigger the effect, until it becomes absurdly strong. This is known as the 'forward guidance puzzle'. Soon enough, however, some studies have included a few twists and frictions to the mainstream model, and the forward guidance puzzle disappears.[19]

Quantitative Easing

Probably the most famous non-standard policy is Quantitative Easing, or 'QE' in common parlance. QE is essentially a central bank purchase of risk free (long-term) assets, most commonly government bonds. The objective of QE is to push down the long end of the yield curve of interest rates, and hence provide further stimulus to the economy over and beyond low short-term interest rates. All major central banks in the world have conducted some type of QE in the wake of the global financial crisis – joining the Bank of Japan who was already a long standing member of the club.

In textbook models, QE should be largely ineffective. At the ZLB, the economy finds itself in a 'liquidity trap', where any additional money put into circulation by the central bank is hoarded and not spent. From a monetary policy point of view, this situation is like walking on a quicksand – with its open market operations, the central bank is essentially swapping two types of equally desirable risk free assets; hence central bank money and Treasury bills are close to perfect substitutes.[20] In this regard, it is convenient to mention Neil Wallace's irrelevance theorem for money market operations and the central bank balance sheet. It shows analytically that in a model with frictionless (perfectly functioning) financial markets it is irrelevant what the central bank has on the asset side of the balance sheet.[21] In its most basic form, therefore, QE is immaterial, what the Germans sometimes unflatteringly call 'Umbuchung' (literally 'transfer of an entry'). And yet, there is evidence that somehow QE works, at least for interest rates and asset prices (for inflation is somewhat less clear). Indeed, the previous Chairman of the Federal Reserve, Ben Bernanke, quipped that 'The problem with QE is it works in practice, but it doesn't work in theory'.

How do we know that it works, and why could it be the case? Most of the evidence on the effects of QE comes from the analysis of surprise announcements of QE policies on a range of financial market prices, say long-term interest rates, equity returns, and exchange rates. This type of evidence, typically called 'event studies', points to significant effects of QE announcements: they tend to lower long-term interest rates, in particular, which is the key objective of the policy. As long as the short-term market reaction (say, daily) is a good indicator of the reaction of the private sector more generally and at longer horizons, say quarterly or yearly, then this evidence does suggest that QE works. However, this is quite a big if. There is some evidence coming from empirical work other than event studies, but this is more limited and less straightforward.[22] The honest answer to the question of whether QE works to stimulate the economy at the zero bound is therefore 'probably, but we are not sure yet'.

Assuming it works, then why? What have QE sceptics missed? There are two transmission channels that are typically put forward by advocates of QE.

First, these policies may have signalling effects, similar to forward guidance. Unlike forward guidance, which can eventually be just cheap talk, QE 'puts the central banker's money where the mouth is'. More specifically, the central bank is bound to lose money if it does not believe in its own words. If it says that it does not desire or expect higher interest rates down the road but later reneges on its promises, it is bound to experience substantial losses on its bond portfolio. Hence its words are likely to be more believed, and forward guidance and QE can actually reinforce each other.

Second, long-term bonds may be imperfect substitutes for bank reserves, i.e. central bank money, what is known as the 'portfolio balance' channel. Long-term bonds have longer maturity and, even when they are seen as risk free at maturity (which is the case for, say, US or German long dated government bonds) the holder still faces substantial 'duration risk', i.e. the risk of experiencing losses if future short-term interest rates rise. Moreover, government bonds may be an asset of choice especially for institutional investors (say, pension funds) or used as collateral in private repurchase agreements between private financial institutions. Creating an artificial scarcity of these bonds through QE may therefore push up their price (and lower their yield) even if the private sector receives central bank money in return. Clearly, this channel hinges on the assumption that government bonds are 'special', over and above the expected yield to maturity that they entail. That may or may not be the case, depending on a host of legal and institutional factors.[23] Therefore, the effects of QE through the portfolio balance channel may be very country-specific and contingent. This transmission channel builds on fickle financial frictions that may, or equally may not, exist in reality.

In this respect, it is useful to make a parallel between the effectiveness of standard and non-standard monetary policies. As seen, 'standard' monetary policy is conducted via loans by the central bank to commercial banks collateralised with assets such as government bonds; non-standard policy, at least in its most typical QE incarnation, means exchanging central bank money with government bonds at various maturities. The economic nature of these exchanges is not that different, after all, but there are important differences in detail that matter given the institutional background. Because QE involves *outright* purchases of government bonds, rather than acquisition of the same bonds as collateral, only QE creates a true scarcity of those bonds.[24] Moreover, the fact that the purchase is outright signals the fact that it is not easily reversed in the future, though this is not necessarily the case in all circumstances.[25] Indeed, the key to the effectiveness of QE is the expectation that it is not quickly reversed in the future; the *current* money supply does not really matter as such. At the same time, these considerations also buttress the view that QE is not really non-standard after all, because there is a close resemblance to the so-called standard monetary policy operations.

There is a growing literature and policy debate on the possible downsides of QE, which are often mixed with concerns related to low interest rates ('low for long'), which we will see more extensively in Chapter 5. There are at least three significant downsides of QE that are typically less relevant or absent in the so-called standard policy.

First, QE acts mainly through asset prices, notably bond, equities and exchange rates. Of course, standard monetary policy also affects those variables, but this is more a side effect rather than the *raison d'être* of the policy, which is the case for

QE. Large swings in asset prices have important distributional consequences, and in particular an increase in asset prices may disproportionately benefit the rich, who typically hold more financial wealth. The literature is however inconclusive on the empirical importance of QE for income and wealth distribution. One possible counter-argument to this criticism is that, to the extent that QE policies foster job creation, they actually benefit the poor more than the rich, because labour income is relatively much more important for the poor. Some have even claimed that these distributional consequences ultimately represent a threat to central bank independence, although I have not seen evidence on this so far.[26]

Second, QE encumbers the central bank balance sheet with government bonds, and that balance sheet may swell to unprecedented heights (see Figure 4.2). This is particularly a problem if the central bank experience balance sheet losses, which may in turn undermine its independence. It is actually even *by design* that the central bank experience balance sheet losses, because if the policy is successful and the economy escapes from the ZLB and low inflation (or deflation), one should expect short-term interest rates to rise over time, which reduces the prices of the government bonds the central bank holds and may lead to severe losses.

Here it is useful to make a short digression on the possibility that a central bank experiences losses, potentially leading to negative capital. The general message here is that, for a central bank, losses are not a main problem as for a private bank or company – equity and debt liabilities are, for a central bank, more an accounting fiction than an economic reality.[27] Under fiat money at least, the central bank can always write a cheque to itself, and thereby repair its balance sheet. Hence, the prospect of losing money is a consideration of secondary importance – in fact, central banks such as the Czech National Bank and the Bank of Israel have operated successfully with negative capital.[28] In theory, therefore, central banks should not care about their profits, if it can be sure that the Treasury is behind it.[29] A recent

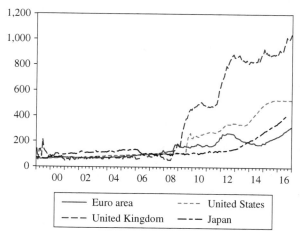

FIGURE 4.2 Size of the central bank balance sheet in main industrialised countries, rescaled at August 2007 = 100.

study looks at the effects of having a positive-profit constraint for the policy choices of the central bank, finding that the constraint leads to distorted choices.[30]

This does not mean, however, that losing money is desirable as it may indeed bring some complications. In fact, another recent study finds that central banks do care for their profits: they are more likely to report small positive profits than small losses, and this propensity is correlated with measures of imperfect central bank independence.[31]

Three of them, in particular, may be a concern.

First, the central bank may need to stray from its inflation target in order to recoup losses (have positive capital) and/or increase the seignorage it gives back to the Treasury, if the latter depends on it for its budgetary situation. Hence negative capital can harm the anti-inflationary credibility of the central bank.

Second, losses and negative capital may make the central bank more dependent on the Treasury to cover its operational expenses, undermining its financial independence. To be fully independent, central banks should send, not receive money from the Treasury. Without the backing of the Treasury, a loss-making central bank can become truly insolvent.

Third, and perhaps most important, loss of taxpayer money is probably not conducive to increasing central bank reputation and the public trust in it – even when the loss is motivated by higher policy objectives.

Therefore, any central bank should have a robust risk management system in place, and prevent losing money while pursuing its policy objectives. So far, the record of central banks is on average pretty good on this count.

Beyond the possibility of losses for the central bank, a third downside of QE is the fact that the central bank purchases a lot of government bonds outright reinforces the *liaison dangereuse* between the central bank and the Treasury, creating moral hazard for the latter. In fact, the Treasury may get used to have its bonds purchased by the central bank and therefore relent on the necessary structural reforms or fiscal consolidation. As far as I know, it has not been established empirically if QE undermines government reform efforts or makes the executive complacent, but it is a question worth investigating and a risk to be kept well in mind.

Helicopter money – or, people's QE

One non-standard policy that typically strikes the imagination of the general public is the so-called 'helicopter money'. The imagery of helicopter money is due to Milton Friedman, who imagined that this type of policy is akin to a helicopter flying over the country and throwing banknotes around. In practice, by helicopter money we mean a version of QE without purchases of government bonds, but a transfer of central bank money to the private sector, directly or indirectly via the government. A popular representation of this policy is the central bank sending cheques, or even banknotes, directly to citizens without any counterpart (not even working in the mean government spending financed by the central bank, i.e. monetary financing).[32] Indeed, some economists have advocated an institutional arrangement whereby monetary and fiscal policy-makers agree on a coordinated monetary-fiscal expansion in a liquidity trap – even though this may be seen as a threat to monetary dominance and central bank independence.[33]

Here it is useful to have another short digression, this time on 'Ricardian equivalence'. When thinking of monetary policy in conjunction with the government budgetary policies and the government balance sheet it is important to point to the importance of Ricardian equivalence – or lack thereof. Ricardian equivalence simply says that any deficit today will fail to stimulate spending because households will internalise the government balance sheet and, more concretely, will know that more government spending today will mean more taxes tomorrow. This view was elaborated by British economist David Ricardo and further developed by others, notably Robert Barro at Harvard University.[34] Ricardian consumers make fiscal policy ineffective, potentially also when in combination with monetary policy.

If consumers are completely Ricardian, then even a combined monetary-fiscal expansion may fail to have significant effects. But there is no reason to be so pessimistic. First, there is ample evidence that consumers are not Ricardian – they have finite lives, liquidity constraints, and so on. Second, helicopter money – if it is believed and consistently implemented – creates net wealth for the private sector in the indefinite future. Even a fully Ricardian consumer would respond to this.

A number of recent papers claim that, under realistic conditions, helicopter money may be more effective than QE, unless expectations react in a particularly unfavourable way.[35] Crucially, a key difference between QE and helicopter money is in the net wealth effect coming from money transfers. Government bonds eventually have to be paid back, while central bank money does not. If this is recognised and believed by the private sector, helicopter money has to be effective to stimulate nominal spending.

The effect, however, is not mechanical and would probably not mainly come from the direct effect of the monetary injection on spending. Unless households are (severely) liquidity constrained, they will not necessarily spend the cheques they receive from the central bank. In fact, if they behave rationally, they will see them as a (nominal) increase in their lifetime wealth and spend only a small part of it, in line with the permanent income hypothesis (namely that consumers in their spending decisions will think about their lifetime wealth, not based on what they earn today). Therefore, the effect of the money transfer on current spending is in principle given by the marginal propensity to consume out of wealth, which is a small number (say, 2%). One would need a very large money transfer to accomplish a material increase in current aggregate demand, or target the transfer to the liquidity constrained households, which would raise very large questions of fairness and distributive justice. In any case, we can forget about cheques to households because nobody in the policy environment has ever seriously considered this possibility. What is worth understanding is the more realistic case of monetary financing, namely higher public spending in deficit, financed by the central bank.

Most of the effectiveness of helicopter money depends on the expectations it creates. At one level, it can be argued that, after all, helicopter money can be conceived as a coordinated fiscal and monetary expansion. In most models, it does not matter much if the monetary easing leg is accomplished through QE or through money transfers. Moreover, if one considers the *aggregate* balance sheet of the Treasury and the central bank, there is really no first order difference between QE and helicopter money. Again, what matters is whether the private sector believes in a permanent increase in the money supply, and one could speculate that the private sector might believe in the permanency of the increase in the money supply more in the case of helicopter money than in the case of QE, which in most cases is construed to be persistent, but not permanent. As for example Simon Wren-Lewis at Oxford University notes, in the end what matters is the private sector belief in the credibility of the central bank inflation target. Even helicopter money will fail to raise prices and economic activity today if the public does not expect it to be permanent. To see this, think of a permanent money transfer that is *expected* to be reversed within one minute; nobody would seriously expect this operation to have a first order impact on the economy. The general lesson is that, in a forward looking model, no monetary policy can 'brute force' the private sector towards any inflation rate – being credible and believed is always a key element of an effective policy.

To be effective, therefore, helicopter money needs to create the expectation or even the commitment that it will not be reversed in the future. Therefore, the effectiveness of these policies depends on the clarity and credibility with which they can be communicated to the public. This is because monetary financing involves a dramatic shift in the policy reaction function. Helicopter money can in fact be written as an interest rate policy rule, but this becomes a rule that has quite different characteristics from a Taylor rule. The private sector may not be used to this different rule, and the impact on expectations may be sluggish – households and firms will take time to understand the new regime and internalise it in their decisions.

For all its promise, helicopter money has a significant political downside and its governance would be burdensome. Central banks may be uncomfortable with helicopter money because it breaks a political taboo – indeed the usual worry with fiat money is to limit its creation rather than foster it, because it can be abused to create high inflation, and our institutions are primed to erect defences against *this* prospect. Expanding the money supply permanently and on purpose and with commitment will take some effort and may be politically unsustainable.[36]

Credit easing policies

Another form of non-standard policy which aims at targeting financial prices other than the short-term interest rate is 'credit easing', which is made out of central bank purchases of risky assets. Under these policies, the central bank swaps central bank money with risky assets, with the aim to lower risk premia and thereby improve financing conditions, over and beyond the effect achieved by (risk free) low short- and long-term interest rates. Note that credit easing policies also break

Wallace's irrelevance principle: the composition of the asset side of the central bank balance sheet matters. In fact, it can be argued that the effectiveness of credit easing policies is based on a less fickle basis than for QE. In this case, the central bank is exchanging a risk free asset, central bank money, for risky assets. This action should mechanically decrease risk premia in almost any model of the economy, and does not depend on the existence of particular frictions as QE does.

A version of credit easing may be described as aiming at correcting market failure in certain markets. The central bank may recognise that, say, the market for car loans may be excessively tight and credit extension in that sector too scarce – say because lenders are worried without reason. The central bank may aim to correct that market failure by purchasing car loans in order to push up their price (and lower yields). The effect of that policy will be larger than intervention in a market where risk premia are 'fair', because the central bank will not only provide aggregate demand stimulus, but will also correct a distortion and improve efficiency in the allocation of resources.

Among the non-standard policies, credit easing is probably the most problematic as it strays too far away from the core task of central banks, which is to steer aggregate demand in a neutral way without favouring a particular sector or actor over another.[37] Distributional questions are best left to elected politicians and are not the competence of the central bank – which also does not possess the information to be able to judge whether a risk premium is fair or not or which market is distorted, especially so if the market is far away from its core competencies (say, not banking but other industries which our central banker does not know well). The risk of losses for the central bank sheet is correspondingly higher than for Quantitative Easing, which is also an additional and important disadvantage. Finally, a further complication is that risky assets are often also more illiquid, and hence harder to value and to sell – hence more work for the central bank staff.

After having explained all the possible downsides, one should also consider that every policy has pros and cons, and it would not be wise to exclude credit easing policies from the armoury of central banks if the associated trade-offs are favourable – say, strong need to stimulate demand at the ZLB, low risk of losses and sectoral distortions.

The surprising stability of inflation

The last decade has seen extraordinary developments from a macroeconomic and especially monetary policy point of view. As was discussed at length so far, after the global financial crisis central banks have implemented policies that were unthinkable only a few years earlier. They have also greatly expanded their balance sheet, leading to a manifold increase in the supply of central bank money.

Against all this, it is quite remarkable that inflation has barely budged after this extraordinary amount of monetary innovation. Figure 4.3 shows annual inflation in the OECD aggregate, with the vertical line marking Lehman. One can see a bit of volatility especially after Lehman, but this mostly reflects movements in oil prices,

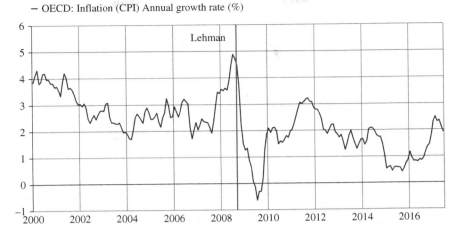

FIGURE 4.3 The remarkable stability of annual CPI inflation in OECD countries. Source: OECD Economic Outlook.

which have a very large short-run effect on consumer prices. Trend inflation appears to have moved very little compared with the pre-crisis environment. It has generally remained on the low side but we have seen neither deflation spiralling out of control – as feared by some – or run-away inflation – as envisaged by others. Clearly, the remarkable stability of inflation needs to be better understood and different interpretations are possible, but it certainly stands as a key fact that begs explanation and which monetary theory needs to confront – for example, the quantity theory does not come out well at all, since very rapid monetary growth has conspicuously failed to create inflation, as noted by John Cochrane, although it is hardly the only theory that is challenged by the post crisis behaviour of inflation.[38]

The Eisler proposal: De-linking unit of account and means of payment

Let us now move to the fifth and last possible solution to the ZLB: the 'de-linking' option. This is normally associated with the name of Robert Eisler, who suggested this option as early as 1932 in his book *Stable Money*, in the middle of the Great Depression.

The rationale behind this idea is relatively straightforward. The ZLB essentially derives from the fact that a medium of exchange (paper banknotes) 'highjacks' the unit of account function of money, where the problem lies. It is therefore reasonable to propose to de-link the two, which should prevent the ZLB problem from arising in the first place. One could imagine prices be set in a 'virtual euro', unencumbered by the ZLB problem, with a floating exchange rate with the 'paper euro' with its undesirable ZLB property. For example, you might go to a shop to buy a TV set worth 1000 'virtual euros' and (if you choose to pay cash) pay 1100 'paper euros' if the exchange rate between the two is 1.1. This would indeed represent a clean solution to the ZLB problem. One can also implement the solution only when the ZLB is a problem, and have paper currency circulate at par with the unit of account otherwise.[39]

Unfortunately, this solution also has significant downsides. As we noted in Chapter 1, there is a reason why the unit of account and the means of payment functions come together; there are in fact important synergies between the two. Breaking the link is therefore bound to come with significant loss of economic efficiency. Why use something as means of payment if this creates transaction costs – especially given that the means of payment exists exclusively to minimise those costs? In practice, establishing a dual system may be tantamount to removing, or at least severely discouraging, the use of cash in the economy, a topic which we will turn to in Chapter 6. There would also be significant transition costs: for example, how to re-define existing contracts, especially if paper currency is legal tender and contracts have been written on it.

In conclusion, the ZLB still looms large for monetary policy, and none of the solutions that we have described in this chapter can be seen as a full and perfect one. Central banks are clearly not powerless at the ZLB, but at the same time it would also be wrong to say that the ZLB does not matter for them or that it does not make their job more difficult. The elimination of paper currency is probably the only clear-cut solution to the ZLB. As long as there are some perceived benefits in having paper currency circulating and low inflation is desirable, it is likely that central banks will continue to struggle with the ZLB problem for years to come – so, stay tuned.

Notes

1. An alternative way to attach an interest rate, positive or negative, to banknotes would be to run a lottery and to give, or withdraw from circulation, banknotes with certain serial numbers. It is clear to see that this, too, would be quite impractical.
2. Menner, M., '"Gesell Tax" and Efficiency of Monetary Exchange', Working Papers Serie AD, Instituto Valenciano de Investigaciones Económica, 2011.
3. Trichet, J.C., 2003, available at https://www.ecb.europa.eu/press/key/date/2003/html/sp031120.en.html.
4. Benhabib, J., Schmitt-Grohe, S. and M. Uribe, 'The Peril with Taylor Rules', *Journal of Economic Theory*, 96, 1–2, 2001, 40–69.
5. See Bullard, J., 'Seven Faces of "The Peril"', *Review, Federal Reserve Bank of St. Louis*, November, 2010, 613–628.
6. Bullard, J., 'Permazero', *Cato Journal* 36, 2, 2016, 415–429.
7. See Garcia Schmidt, M. and M. Woodford, 'Are Low Interest Rates Deflationary? A Paradox of Perfect Foresight Analysis', NBER Working Paper 21614, 2015; they claim that the unintended steady state is not 'learnable', i.e. it is difficult to get there if expectations are adaptive and not rational.
8. The black hole comparison is in Rogoff, K., 'Dealing with Monetary Paralysis at the Zero Bound', *Journal of Economic Perspectives* 31, 3, 2017, 47–66.
9. Eggertsson, G., 'The Paradox of Toil', Federal Reserve Bank of New York Staff Report 433, 2010.

10 One still controversial question is whether fiscal expansion at the ZLB pays for itself, i.e. leads to lower, not higher public debt to GDP ratio. There are more and more indications that this might be so, but still no consensus.
11 See Svensson, L. E. O., 'The Zero Bound in an Open Economy: A Foolproof Way of Escaping from a Liquidity Trap', NBER Working Paper 7957, 2003.
12 This is not entirely uncontroversial, however; see Ascari, G. and A. M. Sbordone, 'The Macroeconomics of Trend Inflation', *Journal of Economic Literature* 52, 3, 679–739.
13 Blanchard, O., Dell'Ariccia, G. and P. Mauro, 'Rethinking Macroeconomic Policy', *Journal of Money, Credit and Banking* 42, 1, 2010, 199–215; Ball, L., 'The Case for 4% Inflation', available at http://voxeu.org/article/case-4-inflation.
14 For a review of price vs. inflation targeting see Vestin, D., 'Price-level versus Inflation Targeting', *Journal of Monetary Economics* 53, 7, 2006, 1361–1376.
15 Berg, C. and L. Jonung, 'Pioneering Price Level Targeting: The Swedish Experience', *Journal of Monetary Economics* 43, 3, 1999, 525–551.
16 The reasoning in this case is not very different from the criticism of the proposal to raise the inflation target.
17 Campbell, J., Evans, C. L., Fisher, J. and A. Justiniano, 'Macroeconomic Effects of Federal Reserve Forward Guidance', *Brookings Papers on Economic Activity* 43, 1, 2012, 1–80.
18 FOMC statement, available at https://www.federalreserve.gov/newsevents/pressreleases/monetary20121212a.htm.
19 McKay, A., Nakamura, E. and J. Steinsson, 'The Power of Forward Guidance Revisited', *American Economic Review* 106, 10, 2016, 3133–3158.
20 Eggertson, G. and M. Woodford, 'The Zero Bound on Interest Rates and Optimal Monetary Policy', *Brookings Papers on Economic Activity* 34, 1, 2003, 139–235.
21 Wallace, N., 'A Modigliani-Millen Theorem for Open Market Operations', *American Economic Review* 71, 3, 1981, 267–274.
22 See Beck, R., Duca, I. and L. Stracca, 'Doctor, Give Me some QE! Treatment and Side Effects of Quantitative Easing', mimeo, 2017.
23 Moreover, QE critics point to the fact that, if government bonds are special for a selected type of agents, their QE-induced scarcity should matter only for them, and not for the economy at large.
24 Some central banks mitigate this scarcity, in particular in terms of available collateral for private sector transactions, by re-lending the government bonds that they acquire through QE. These operations are called 'securities lending'.
25 In theory, standard monetary policy could be conducted through repurchase agreements of government bonds. Central banks could exchange central bank money with government bonds, and promise to buy back the government bonds at a future date. If we see standard monetary policy in this way, the key difference with QE is in the expected duration of the operation. If the purchase is 'outright' the private sector might expect it not to be easily reversed.
26 See de Haan, J. and S. Eijffinger, 'The Politics of Central Bank Independence', Tilburg University Discussion Paper 2016-047, 2016.
27 See for example E. Lonergan, 'Does the Central Bank's Balance Sheet Matter', 25 May 2015, at https://www.philosophyofmoney.net/does-the-central-banks-balance-sheet-matter/.
28 See B. Eichengreen and B. Weder di Mauro, 'Central Banks and the Bottom Line', 12 February 2015, at https://www.project-syndicate.org/commentary/central-bank-balance-sheet-losses-by-barry-eichengreen-and-beatrice-weder-di-mauro-2015-02?barrier=accessreg.
29 Hall, R. E., and R. Reis, 'Maintaining Central-Bank Solvency under New-Style Central Banking', NBER Working Paper 21173, 2015.
30 Berriel, T. and S. Bhattarai, 'Monetary Policy and Central Bank Balance Sheet Concerns', *The B.E. Journal of Macroeconomics*, 9, 1, 2009, 1–33.
31 Goncharov, I., Ioannidou, V. and M. Schmalz, '(Why) Do Central Banks Care about their Profits?', CESIFO Working Papers 6546, 2017.

32 Note that in the European Union monetary financing is explicitly ruled out by Article 123 of the Lisbon Treaty.
33 See S. Wren Lewis, 'Helicopter Money', 22 October 2014, at https://mainlymacro.blogspot.de/2014/10/helicopter-money.html.
34 Barro, R., 'Are Government Bonds Net Wealth?', *Journal of Political Economy* 82, 6, 1974, 1095–1117.
35 Gali, J., 'The Effects of a Money Financed Fiscal Stimulus', Universitat Pompeu Fabra Economics Working Papers 1441, 2016; Buiter, W., 'The Simple Analytics of Helicopter Money: Why it Works – Always', *Economics* 8, 2014–28, 2014; Turner, A., 'The Case for Monetary Finance: An Essentially Political Issue', paper presented at the 16th Jacques Polak Annual Research Conference, 2015.
36 Turner (op. cit.).
37 Hence it is common to say that credit easing policies are a form of 'quasi fiscal policy' – however I am not even sure of what this term actually means; it seems more of a semantic distinction.
38 Cochrane, J., 'The Neo-Fisherian question', 6 November 2014, available at http://johnhcochrane.blogspot.de/2014/11/the-neo-fisherian-question.html.
39 Agarwal, R. and M. Kimball, 'Breaking through the Zero Lower Bound', IMF Working Paper 15/224, 2015.

5

FINANCIAL STABILITY AND THE LENDER OF LAST RESORT FUNCTION OF CENTRAL BANKS

According to the American economist Hyman Minsky, the financial sector is subject to an endogenous cycle of booms and busts. In good times, credit is extended more easily (e.g. at lower interest rates and/or with fewer covenants), borrowing increases and, crucially, credit risk is underestimated. Banks' balance sheets expand and asset prices, in particular house prices, go up. Sooner or later, the moment arrives when expectations suddenly turn and credit risk is revised upwards. Excess euphoria gives way to panic, and the cycle reverses in an abrupt and costly way. The moment the cycle turns is sometimes called the 'Minsky Moment' after Minsky, although the basic idea belongs to other economists too, for example Charles Kindleberger, the author of the book *Manias, Panics, and Crashes*.

Minsky's and Kindleberger's ideas have largely been shelved for decades before enjoying a resurrection after the global financial crisis. Hyman Minsky (1919–1996) certainly was not a household name, and in my career in central banks, I do not recall having heard anybody mentioning his name before 2008. But now, any archive of economics publications or working papers will show that dozens of papers have been written in the past decade with at least some reference to Minsky's ideas – in fact, *not being familiar* with Minsky is now seen as a sign of being somewhat passé!

However, while he is fashionable now, we are still far from having a good understanding of the kind of endogenous instability that Minsky described. A lot of work is ongoing to unravel the mysteries of the 'financial cycle', as it is now called, both in central banks and outside.[1]

One of the purported characteristics of the financial cycle is the role of outside money, which directly implicates the central bank. In the boom phase of the cycle there is little demand for central bank money, and the money multiplier (the ratio between inside and outside money, say between bank deposits and central bank money) is high. In the terminology of the hierarchy of money, inside money (notably bank liabilities) and outside money are close substitutes. This reverses in the panic phase, when private agents flock to outside money, and the distance between inside and outside money rises exponentially. This is where central banks are left with the question of how to steer the supply of outside money in a panic situation. This concerns both a systemic crisis, when all banks are affected, and a crisis of an individual institution, where it is the distance between the liabilities of a particular bank and outside money that is growing.

Generally speaking, central banks have four roles to play in financial stability, and we will go through all of them in this chapter. First, they provide lender of last resort funding, which essentially implies accommodating the higher demand for outside money in panic periods. Second, they need to be aware that their control of inflation can have financial stability implications, through two mechanisms that we will describe (debt deflation and the financial accelerator). Third, central banks may themselves put financial stability at risk and stoke the financial cycle, by keeping interest rates too low for too long, although, as we will soon see, this is still rather controversial. Fourth, central banks have to play a stabilisation role on inflation depending on the vagaries of the financial cycle. When the financial cycle is in the upward phase, growth and inflation tend to go up, and the reverse is true in the low phase of the cycle, especially if it is punctuated by crises. In any case, central banks do need to be aware of financial stability questions and, as the global financial crisis had made painfully clear, they ignore them at their peril.

What is financial stability?

Before we plunge into the role of central banks, it is useful to pause to consider the definition of financial stability. That definition is not as straightforward as that of price stability (although even this is not as simple as it is commonly thought). The best way to think about financial stability is a situation where the financial system performs its function of intermediating savings and investment in a normal way, for example the interest rates charged to risky borrowers are within the usual distance from the risk free interest rate; more in jargon, 'credit spreads' are at 'normal' levels. (Credit spreads are the difference between the interest rate paid by a typical risky borrower and the risk free rate.) Therefore, even a very inefficient or underdeveloped financial system can be stable, and it might even be the case that too much stability is detrimental to long-term growth.[2] This notion of stability is related to the idea that financial intermediation behaves within the range that can be expected based on historical experience, and does not deviate too much from it. A recurrent theme in financial instability episodes is that debt contracts are either not fully honoured or there is a widespread perception that they could not be honoured. In this case, one could think that a legitimate expectation is that debt contracts are paid back, as this is after all typically enshrined in law, whereas widespread defaults on debt contracts are outside the normal range of behaviour and therefore marks of financial instability.

In my opinion, the closest to an operational measure of financial stability that we have available now is some indicator of default risk for banks, because banks play a crucial role in financial intermediation (more on this later). Moreover, banks can be seen as a bundle of a debt contract (the liabilities of their balance sheet) and a risky asset (the assets side of their balance sheet). They normally face fluctuations in the value of risky assets, but they are solvent as long as they can honour the debt contracts in their liabilities side. Therefore, an abnormal value for the aggregate default risk of banks is probably a good aggregate indicator of financial instability. However, we should keep in mind that a low reading for bank default risk is not necessarily a signal that everything is in order – in fact, in financial stability matters (as in other fields of human activity arguably) problems tend to breed in good times, so central banks and regulators can never really relax.

Credit matters

In a well-developed economy producing complex and durable goods there is a good number of transactions that do require credit. In general, whenever there is a distance in time between purchase and payment, some form of credit is necessary. Here we define credit as the temporary transfer of real purchasing power between two households or firms, to be paid back in time and possibly with interest.

For example, it makes economic sense that payment for housing is temporally separated from consuming housing services. A young person has a high demand for housing services but not yet the resources to pay for them, and needs to accumulate them over her lifetime. For that reason, the housing market could hardly exist without credit. This is an important consideration because it shows that, if credit provision is impaired, an entire set of transactions becomes impossible, and economic activity eventually has to shrink. In fact, during financial crises investment and durable goods, i.e. the sectors of the economy that mostly depend on credit, are the first to fall and the slowest to recover.

Financial intermediation is paramount for the provision of credit. In an ideal world without frictions there is no need for financial intermediation and credit can be provided directly. If I produce a durable good, I can provide credit to the purchaser and be paid back in time. Unfortunately, the purchaser can walk away with the good without paying back or refuse to pay back for other reasons – the result of which is that this transaction can eventually never take place. Providing credit in a modern economy requires professional expertise from financial intermediaries and a functioning legal and judicial system, which together form the financial system. Financial intermediaries and the financial system play an important allocative function, because they decide who receives credit and who doesn't, which is particularly important for investment. As a result of actions by financial intermediaries some investments are made (say, developing a new aeroplane) while others aren't (say, developing a new drug), it is for that reason that the financial system is sometimes called 'the brain of the economy'.[3]

Credit is largely debt

In principle, credit is a real phenomenon which reflects the fact that for some transactions purchase and payment have to happen at different points in time. As a matter of principle, there is nothing inherently *monetary* in credit provision. In practice, however, most of credit is nominal debt, i.e. debt denominated in monetary terms. This is the main reason why central banks are important for credit provision and money and credit are closely related.

Broadly speaking, we can distinguish between two forms of credit, from the standpoint of the borrower: debt and equity (there are also hybrid forms which should not concern us for now). A key characteristic of debt is that, at least in principle, it has to be paid back in full, while the return on equity depends on the returns on investment.[4] Suppose that I develop an investment project which has two possible rates of return, one high and one low (say, negative). Further, suppose that the probability of experiencing the high return is a function both of my effort (that is costly for me) and luck, and that the lender is not able to disentangle the two (and probably neither am I).

In theory, the best form of financing for my project is through equity. In this way, the lender and I share the risks of the enterprise, and hence the unavoidable turns of luck. Moreover, my incentives are in the right place because I will gain or lose from the investment and have an incentive to spend effort for the success of the enterprise. The lender, in turn, has to 'put his money where his mouth is', and he will be careful to provide equity only to worthwhile investment projects, where the probability of success is high, with positive consequences for allocative efficiency.

However, we observe that most of credit is debt, and equity does not play a material role in the financing of investment, especially in net terms (firms often buy back their shares). There are several reasons for this. First, it is far easier to steal or divert equity than debt. If I can divert the resources obtained through equity financing to my private use, claiming a streak of bad luck, I can be privately better off at the expense of the lender who may never find out. Second, and related, while risk sharing is in principle efficient, in the presence of *asymmetric information* (i.e., the borrower has more information on the project than the lender) it may be preferable that risks are borne by the borrower, who is the most likely to observe and control them by spending effort. Third, equity financing implies monitoring costs for the lender, at all times, precisely because the lender has to understand what part of the investment return is due to luck and what to quality and effort of the borrower. Given all these frictions, it may be preferable for the lender to offer a debt contract which has to be paid back with a pre-determined rate of return at the beginning, and which can be defaulted on only in the low return state, in which case the investment project is audited (to make sure that resources were not diverted or stolen). One key advantage of debt over equity is that monitoring costs are incurred *only in the bad state of the world* and not at all times. This theory of debt is known as 'costly state verification' or CSV, and may help to explain why debt is so pervasive, in particular in situations where asymmetric information is largest, for example in the international setting.[5]

There may certainly be other, and less theoretically compelling or defensible, reasons for the prevalence of debt. One is the distortion induced by the tax system, which in many countries treats the interest on debt as a cost to be deducted from taxable income, while capital gains from equity investment are not. Part of this distortion arises from the willingness of public authorities to favour mortgage lending in particular and thereby foster home ownership, which may have its own independent and sometimes non-economic advantage (say, social cohesion). It is important to address these distortions and to analyse them in a critical way, but the point remains valid that normally there is fundamental reason why debt contracts exist, and that the CSV logic provides a powerful incentive for credit to be offered as a debt contract.

However, debt contracts do have an important downside: they are at the root of all financial instability. Precisely because debt contracts are typically paid back most of the time, defaulting on debt is typically a traumatic experience which involves costs and disruption. In the CSV frame of thinking, financial instability can arise both *ex ante*, because lenders anticipate a high risk of default and hence have to pay the monitoring costs, and *ex post*, if a high default rate actually leads to large monitoring and auditing costs. In general, it is almost impossible to have financial instability with equity, while all financial instability derives from – it is a side effect of – debt contracts.

Credit is largely nominal debt

The other dimension that needs explaining is why credit is almost always *nominal* debt – namely, defined in terms of central bank money and hence giving the central bank a central role. Again, in theory at least, debt contracts could be written in real terms, for example in terms of consumption goods and/or indexed to inflation. In practice, this rarely happens, in particular in the private sector (some government debt is indexed to inflation, although even there most of it is not). There have been various attempts in the literature to justify the ubiquitous nature of nominal debt, but it is fair to say that we still don't have a single compelling explanation. Probably the theory that is closest to explaining this fact is based on the idea that inflation is costly to observe or observed with delay,[6] and/or that it is not easy to incorporate indexation in simple debt contracts. For government debt specifically, it has been argued that nominal debt may be desirable because of the positive correlation between inflation and government spending. With nominal debt we obtain a situation where high inflation is helpful (by reducing the real value of debt) exactly when government spending soars - say, in a war. This reduces tax distortions, as taxes would have to be high to pay for ballooning government spending.[7] Other authors have suggested that, for banks, nominal deposit contracts are optimal in terms of limiting real risks for banks.[8]

Financial intermediation

Credit can be provided directly (direct finance) or indirectly through financial intermediaries. The way in which credit is provided depends a lot on the characteristics of the borrower. If the borrower can release a lot of information on himself and/or the investment project that he intends to finance, he can convince lenders to provide credit without resorting to a financial intermediary such as a bank. For smaller and less sophisticated investors, say households and small firms, this is typically not possible and for that reason these agents almost never issue financial liabilities such as bonds; all their credit comes through banks, who are specialised in providing it and work by large numbers to diversify risks.

More generally, one can think that there are fixed costs in lending contracts, which is probably the case for both debt and equity contracts. This in turn suggests the existence of economies of scale and therefore the optimality of concentrating financial intermediation with professional intermediaries.

Historically, modern banks arose in mediaeval and early Renaissance Italy, in particular in the rich cities of the centre-north such as Florence and Venice. Indeed, the word 'bank' comes from the Italian 'banco', which means table or desk. The most ancient bank still in existence is, according to most accounts, the Monte dei Paschi di Siena, whose headquarters are in the Tuscan town of Siena, Italy and which has been operating continuously since 1472. Its magnificent headquarters in Siena and its illustrious history conceal the fact that its recent history has been more troubled.

There is quite a consensus amongst economic historians that banks initially evolved from the activity of money changing, in particular exchanging used coins. Of course, in those times coins were much less reliable and more easily debased than nowadays, and were, overall, a quite inefficient payment method. A banker who knew how to evaluate the coins and was ready to store and exchange them was, not surprisingly, much in demand. From the activity of storing and exchanging coins the opening of paper accounts from clients (including overdrafts) was a natural step, and a very successful one. Nowadays, most payments are done through the books of the banks and banknotes and coins are typically used only for small purchases.

The raison d'être for the existence of the banks is therefore mainly the production of bank deposits, not lending. The activity of long-term lending to borrowers, and gathering information about them, that we typically associate with banks came only much later, in the 19th century during the Second Industrial Revolution.

An enduring legacy of the original activity of banks – storing and exchanging coins – is that banks need to have good vaults and be perceived to be strong and safe, as well as have a reputation for seriousness and integrity. Indeed, a major concern in earlier times must have been that clients' coins were either stolen by outsiders or appropriated by a dishonest banker. Still nowadays, banks are typically very bulky and solid places (the highrises that we often see in financial centres), and bankers strive for a reputation of integrity.

Bank deposits and liquidity creation

The familiar bank deposit has real centre stage in the development of the banking sector, and still plays a very important role nowadays. The distinctive characteristic of bank deposits is that they can always be redeemed, i.e. converted into cash, at par. They are therefore the most 'plain vanilla' financial instrument that can be conceived, from the standpoint of the depositors. Because of this characteristic and also of the development of electronic means such as bank transfers and cards allowing the portability of deposits, which allow us to walk around with our bank deposit virtually in our pockets, they have become widespread as means of exchange. Over recent decades deposit insurance has also become ubiquitous, which further reinforces the commoditisation of deposits.

It is possible to measure the liquidity creation of banks by comparing the amount of liquid liabilities that they produce, mainly bank deposits, and the amount of illiquid assets they hold, mainly loans. This is banks' 'liquidity transformation', a situation where a collection of assets is repackaged and the resulting instruments have higher liquidity than the original assets. Note that this function is conceptually separate from, even though certainly not independent of, the risk transformation function that banks also perform (safe liabilities, risky assets).

There are estimates on how much liquidity the banking system creates. In a recent study, the authors classify banks' asset and liabilities as liquid, semi-liquid or illiquid (also accounting for off-balance sheet items). According to their preferred measure, the US banking system created liquidity for about 2.8 trillion US dollars, which was about four and a half times bank capital; liquidity creation is also found to have grown significantly over time, despite ongoing bank dis-intermediation in the US.[9]

Crucial in the management of bank deposits is the fact that deposit withdrawals are not perfectly correlated and are predictable in large numbers. In this way, the bank can go on with relatively little cash reserves. However, the flip side of this otherwise efficient arrangement is that the bank is vulnerable to coordinated withdrawals of deposits. To keep things simple, let's suppose a bank has only ten clients. Normally, these clients withdraw cash from their deposit accounts in an uncoordinated fashion, so that the bank does not need to have a lot of cash to satisfy them. If the probability for each client to withdraw half of their holdings is 10%, the probability that all of them do that at the same time is close to zero. If however each client withdraws cash when others decide to do so, the bank has a problem. If the bank does not have enough cash reserves or capital, it can go bankrupt very rapidly.

Banks have high leverage

The fact that banks have fixed value liabilities implies that they also have a lot of leverage, defined as the ratio between their total assets and their equity liabilities – loosely speaking, high leverage means having a lot of debt to finance risky assets. Banks have typically much higher leverage than most other firms. For example, a car producer may have a leverage ratio between two and three, whereas it is common for a bank to have leverage of 20 or more. High leverage is good for shareholders because, on average, risky assets have higher returns than fixed liabilities, due to risk premia. Therefore, the return on equity is higher, the higher the leverage. Of course, the potential for losing is correspondingly higher, but this is a limited problem for the shareholders.

Indeed, banks – like most other firms – are characterised by *limited liability*; shareholders can gain, but cannot lose, at least not more than they have invested. At this stage we might pause to consider whether limited liability is a good idea at all. The first thing to note about limited liability is that it is a relatively recent legal concept, well established only since the 19th century, where it was introduced in English law. The reader may remember that, in Shakespeare's *The Merchant of Venice*, Shylock demand a pound of flesh as a guarantee for his loan. Limited liability essentially says that a person's liability is limited by a fixed sum, not by his or her whole net worth, let alone his or her body or freedom.

The main advantage of limited liability is that it encourages entrepreneurship. Because the downside is more limited, the reasoning goes, people may be more willing to undertake risky projects, with a high probability to fail but also with the greatest potential when they do not. The biggest downside of limited liability is that it may make people too risk loving, because they gain more than they lose if risk is higher – especially if somebody else, for example the taxpayer, will ultimately bear the brunt of losses. Countries are also different in their acceptance of limited liability in financial contracts. Mortgages, for example, are typically 'no recourse' (liability is limited to the collateral, i.e. the real estate purchased) in the US, but not in Europe, where borrowers are liable with their income and wealth too.

Limited liability is one key reason why banks are regulated.[10] Bank shareholders would increase the return on their capital by simply increasing risk, due to limited liability. The regulators know this, and impose minimal capital requirements, which is another way to limit leverage and risk taking.

Run, run

The fact that banks are fragile (short-term fixed liabilities, long-term risky assets) implies that they may be subject to runs. This is a recurrent theme in economic history, as we will soon see, and may be the most important reason for the existence of central banks.

The possibility of runs depends on the fact that early liquidation of long-term assets destroys value. Think of a house being built over two years, financed by rolling over one-year debt. At the end of the first year, the lender decides, for any apparently irrelevant reason (say, the emergence of a 'sunspot') that it is too risky to lend and withdraws the financing. (A 'sunspot' in macroeconomics is a general term for an irrelevant event which however makes agents focus on one or another equilibrium, in a situation where multiple equilibria are possible. In this case, the possible equilibria are the 'run' (bad) and 'no run' (good) equilibria.) The developer has therefore to liquidate, i.e. sell, the half-built house. Of course, a half-built house is worth practically nothing, so the early liquidation reduces value – actually, it may bankrupt the developer. Ironically, this validates the initial belief of the lender, who feels vindicated from the failure that the project was actually doomed from the beginning.

We therefore have two possible equilibria: either the debt is rolled over at the end of the first year, and everything goes well, or it is not, and the developer goes bankrupt. This is known in the profession as the Diamond and Dybvig model, from the 1983 paper where this mechanism was rigorously described.[11] The reason why this mechanism is called 'run' is precisely because, once it is initiated, the earlier you withdraw your funds, the higher the probability that you are paid back in full. Often depositors and other holders of short-term debt literally run for their savings.

An additional complication is given by the so-called 'fire sale externality'. If the assets that are being liquidated in haste have a market price, that action alone will depress the price also for other borrowers ('fire sale' prices), even those who did not experience problems with rolling over their debt. For example, bank A holds a lot of, say, commercial real estate loans and is subject to a run. The hasty liquidation of its assets reduces the price of that asset, with the consequence that holdings of the same asset by bank B are less valuable now, even if the bank is perfectly safe and sound. Therefore, a run on one intermediary may make other intermediaries insolvent and spark contagion.

The pure model of a bank run involves multiple equilibria for no apparent reason, what in the economics literature is called 'sunspot equilibria'. A perfectly solvent and healthy bank can be driven to bankruptcy. In reality, the truth is somewhere in the middle; bank runs are always initiated where there is at least a whiff of information that the concerned bank may be in trouble. That does not mean, of course, that all runs are fully justified by fundamentals. It is the same with viruses and bacteria: they are more likely to attack the sick than the healthy – which, of course, does not imply that one should let the sick die.

One important downside of a bank run is that either the bank or, worse, the financial system as a whole is forced to do an inefficiently rapid de-leveraging, which in turn can severely impair credit creation (credit crunch). Moreover, bank liabilities (deposits) are used as inside money, so a contraction in bank balance sheets may also reduce the money supply. A striking example of the primary importance of this mechanism – and indeed of the importance of financial intermediation in a modern economy – is the Great Depression of the 1930s.

Bank fragility and liquidity: a necessary trade-off?

Banks' vulnerability to runs is often seen as a shortcoming which needs to be prevented and corrected via public regulation. But is it necessarily bad from the standpoint of liquidity creation?

The first thing to notice is that bank runs as a pure expectations-driven phenomenon independent of fundamentals have been relatively rare in history. In most cases, there has been some kind of real risk of insolvency for the bank being victim of a run. It is true that a run can precipitate the insolvency of a financial intermediary which could otherwise have been avoided; but the run is rarely the only or even main cause of the bankruptcy of the bank: it is rather typically an amplification mechanism. However, it can still be undesirable even only as amplification channel.

The mirror image of banks' fragility is their ability to create liquidity and there is a trade-off between these two dimensions. Society needs to choose the best point in this trade-off. Requiring banks to entirely cover their deposit base with reserves, the so-called 'narrow banking', solves the trade-off by minimising the risk of runs, but also constrains liquidity creation. Fractional reserve banking, where banks only hold a small fraction of reserves to back up their liabilities, is a solution which greatly enhances liquidity production, at the cost of a higher risk of runs. So far, most countries have opted for the latter model, but there have been several proposals to move the system towards narrow banking and some of them have been part of the regulatory overhaul following the 2007–09 global financial crisis. Notably, banks are now subject to a liquidity ratio, whereby they need to hold a sufficient amount of liquid assets against their liabilities. Although it is not a complete shift to narrow banking, it is certainly a move in that direction. Moreover, as an enduring result of non-standard monetary policies banks are now holding many more reserves than they used to, which is a key safeguard against instability and runs. Some central banks, on their part, have started paying interest on reserves, so as to reduce the cost for banks to hold reserves. Over the long term, one of the important questions is whether this situation of 'excess' reserves will persist in the post-crisis environment and if this is desirable from a financial stability perspective.

Yes, we did it. We're very sorry. But thanks to you, we won't do it again.

With these words, Ben Bernanke, later Chairman of the US Federal Reserve Board, concluded his speech at the conference in honour of Milton Friedman in 2002 – some five years before the global financial crisis.

It was an extraordinary testimony to the lifelong work of Milton Friedman and Anna Schwartz, who, in their monumental *A Monetary History of the United States*, laid the responsibility of the greatest economic catastrophe of the twentieth century, the Great Depression of 1929–1933, at the feet of the Federal Reserve.[12] Indeed they wrote that 'the contraction is in fact a tragic testimonial to the importance of monetary forces'. During the Great Depression, which started in the United States, US money supply contracted by about a third under the Federal Reserve watch. The first year of recession had in fact been just a 'normal' fall in private consumption following the stock market crash.[13] However, starting from 1930 a series of banking panics sparked a sharp decline in the money supply and a credit crunch (a severe reduction of credit availability). Banking panic was ended only with the banking holiday ordered by the Roosevelt administration in the winter of 1933. There is now a wide consensus around Friedman and Schwartz's views that the Federal Reserve failed to provide adequate liquidity to the banking system was at a minimum a key aggravating factor transforming a normal recession into the Great Depression.

The Federal Reserve failed to stem the reduction in the money supply probably not only due to the Gold Standard still in place at the time,[14] especially at the beginning, but also by 'ineptitude and fear', or maybe deadlock and indecision. Moreover, past experience in high inflation shaped in part the response to the Depression in the 1930s, in the US and elsewhere.[15]

Part of the reason for the Federal Reserve inaction was institutional – the Federal Reserve was not an independent institution, and the Secretary of the Treasury at the time, Andrew Mellon, was a convinced 'liquidationist' – he believed that bank failures were ultimately beneficial, pruning the economy of weak institutions – 'purge the rottenness out of the system'.[16] The Federal Reserve Chairman, Eugene Meyer, was readier to intervene and was in fact instrumental at a later stage in developing a doctrine of federal intervention in financial rescues – but this was a view that was clearly in a minority in 1929.[17]

Thus, the Great Depression was largely a run on bank deposits, not effectively countered by the Federal Reserve. The 2007–2009 global financial crisis was also a run, this time on non-bank financial intermediaries. However, this time central banks around the world acted much more forcefully – they heeded the lesson of the Great Depression, and at least in part avoided another one.

In fact, a key difference between the Great Depression of 1929–1933 and the global financial crisis of 2007–09 was the strikingly different policy response.[18] This was partly due to higher automatic stabilisers in place in the 2000s.[19] A more active use of fiscal policy, in particular, was motivated by the notion that this policy is more potent when the banking system is impaired and interest rates are at the zero lower bound.[20]

The lender of last resort (LROR) function

What can economic public policy do in order to prevent or mitigate bank runs? Especially after the Great Depression, several countries introduced legislation to reduce the risk of bank runs. A key innovation was deposit insurance: small depositors, up to a certain threshold, are insured against the default of a bank.[21] This is a key defence against bank runs, which proved its worth during the global financial crisis.

However, deposit insurance helps protect against runs only up to a point. Especially when the banking system becomes very large, no insurance can effectively deal with a run on the entire system. Moreover, depositors and other creditors of a bank can still run if they doubt that insurance will be sufficient or full – in most cases with some reason. Finally, some bank liabilities (large deposits, non-deposit liabilities) are typically excluded from deposit insurance. Hence the key defence against bank runs is ultimately the existence of a Lender of Last Resort: somebody who lends to banks in a panic and who is immune from it. In most countries, the entity playing this role is the central bank.

Why central banks?

Here we should recall that central bank money stands at the apex of the 'hierarchy of money' – a run on inside money is essentially a run towards outside money. A key element of financial stability is indeed the confidence in redemption of bank liabilities into outside money – and indeed that confidence is the first to go in a banking crisis. The central bank, with its deep pockets in outside money, is uniquely placed to provide LOLR. The central bank by definition cannot experience a liquidity crisis, and it is even questionable if they can ever experience a solvency crisis. At the same time, central banks should be doing LOLR carefully and deliberately: they should not abuse this power and thereby create moral hazard. (In economics, moral hazard denotes a situation when somebody takes on more risk than is considered optimal, knowing that he will be protected by the consequences as risks are shared. For example, I can neglect fire precautions if I know I have fire insurance – this would be moral hazard.)

Until the global financial crisis, the LOLR function was relatively little known among monetary economists and received little attention. In particular, it was widely considered to be relevant mostly for individual banks, not for the system as a whole, at least in rich countries. As a consequence, the LOLR function was not part of the typical curriculum in macroeconomics – indeed Sir Paul Tucker, then Deputy Governor at the Bank of England, lamented that 'the relative neglect of LOLR in the core literature of central banking over the past 20 years is a tragedy'.[22]

The main economic rationale of the LOLR function is that a public authority, the central bank, takes a position against the market in a situation of market failure, i.e. when the interbank market does not work properly. This is a difficult function because it requires taking a stance on whether there is a market failure, and is typically more difficult than standard monetary policy. I tend to agree with Willem Buiter when he writes that:

> Making monetary policy under conditions of orderly markets is really not that hard. Any group of people with IQs in three digits (individually) and familiar with (almost) any intermediate macroeconomics textbook could do the job. Dealing with a liquidity crisis and credit crunch is hard. Inevitably, it exposes the central bank to significant financial and reputational risk. The central banks will be asked to take credit risk (of unknown) magnitude onto their balance sheets and they will have to make explicit judgments about the creditworthiness of various counterparties. But without taking these risks the central banks will be financially and reputationally safe, but poor servants of the public interest.[23]

The most difficult aspect of LOLR is that it is necessary to distinguish, in real time, illiquidity and insolvency. LOLR funding should be provided to illiquid but fundamentally solvent institutions. More often than not, this is a very difficult choice to make, as the boundary between illiquidity and insolvency is often blurred.

The Bagehot doctrine

After having established that there is a valid reason for central banks to become lenders of last resort, the next question is then: How to do it?

For some curious reason, in this domain most of the doctrine dates back to the early to mid-19th century and has not evolved much since. The LOLR doctrine is mostly associated with the name of Walter Bagehot, although the intellectual roots of his position date back to Henry Thornton before him.[24] Even nowadays, every central banker conducting a lender of last resort operation pays at least lip service to the famous Bagehot dictum inspired by his book *Lombard Street*: 'lend freely, against good collateral and at a penalty rate'.

The "lend freely" part of the dictum is the easiest to understand. It is another way to say that the central bank should be lending in a panic and take the opposite position to the market, which is in a state of panic. It is about correcting a market failure that manifests itself in inefficient runs.

'Against good collateral'? Here it gets harder. We have already seen in Chapter 3 that collateral policy is a material element of modern monetary policy. The fact that monetary policy operations are against collateral says very little on how to do LOLR. What Bagehot – or maybe his modern interpretation – is saying is that the central bank should lend against 'intrinsically good' collateral, namely collateral that would be good under the 'no run' equilibrium, but that may be impaired or poorly valued in a panic. Recall, in a run bank assets are valued at fire sale prices, not at fair value – the central bank in its LOLR role should not consider collateral like the private sector, at fire sales value, but at its intrinsic value. Clearly, another additional consideration to be kept in mind is that collateral in central bank lending to commercial banks serves the purpose of protecting the central bank balance sheet and avoiding direct money transfers. Nowhere is this concern more important than in a bank panic – so the central bank may also want to be prudent in its collateral valuation. For example, it may want to take the collateral at fair value, but then apply a higher haircut to it. It is a difficult call to make, because in this case minimising risks for the central bank balance sheet may be incompatible with the fundamental aim to counter the panic. For this reason, central bank decisions on collateral are frequency criticised, in and out of crises.[25]

What about the penalty rate? This is perhaps the most controversial element of the Bagehot doctrine and it is not even sure what Bagehot really meant with it – in fact he did not even mention the word 'penalty' which was later widely used by his readers.[26] What a penalty rate may mean is that LOLR loans to banks are made with a higher interest rate than normal monetary policy operations, in order to discourage its excessive use and stoke moral hazard. On the other hand, a higher penalty might in fact discourage moral hazard, but lower the effectiveness of LOLR – or prevent commercial banks from using the LOLR facilities, with a negative externality for other banks. Think of the following example: flu shots may make people less responsible in trying to avoid getting a virus (moral hazard), but getting the shots may also be in the public interest to prevent the spread of contagion.

As a matter of fact, a penalty rate is not always applied in LOLR operations. Again, it is a difficult call to make, which requires judgement.

Historical evolution of the LOLR

The first central bank to make extensive use of the LOLR is, not surprisingly, the Bank of England – indeed it is in England that the LOLR doctrine developed, as we have seen.

Before the creation of the Federal Reserve, clearinghouses partly played the role of a lender of last resort quite effectively between 1865 and 1914 in the United States.[27] However, they did not so to a full extent and the national banking era is littered with banking crises. Private clearinghouses tended to defend the interests of the members, not the public interest. This eventually led to the creation of the Federal Reserve in 1913.

Nowadays, almost all main central banks see the LOLR function as one main central banking function. One frequent question is whether it is beneficial if the central bank is also the regulator and/or supervisor of the banking system for the LOLR function – should supervision and LOLR be under the same roof? As usual in economics, there are trade-offs associated with this choice. On one hand, it is beneficial if the central bank has enough information on the state of the banking system or of individual banks – it may help in making the right call between illiquidity and insolvency. On the other hand, there is also the concrete risk of a conflict of interest: for example, the LOLR function may pressure the supervisory arm to 'window dress' its assessment of a particular bank in favour of, say, illiquidity vs. insolvency.

Why not leave it to the interbank market?

A need for LOLR assumes a market failure in the interbank market – in principle, it should be up to the interbank market to do a proper risk sharing of 'liquidity shocks' – think of them as random transformations of inside into outside money due to shifts in creditors' trust in banks. If the interbank market works properly, there is no reason to have LOLR for *individual* banks – if anything the LOLR should only concern the system as a whole – in jargon, it is about the central bank accommodating *aggregate* 'velocity shocks' (shocks shifting the demand away from inside money towards central bank money).[28]

But the market is also not good at disentangling liquidity and solvency in real time. Here a characteristic of credit markets that is normally not shared by other markets comes into play: in credit markets, a lower price can actually *reduce*, not increase demand. In the market for, say, apples, a lower price normally fosters demand. If people become less willing to eat apples, the price falls to clear the market – perhaps it will just take a bit of time if prices are sticky. But in markets characterised by a lot of asymmetric information, this may not necessarily happen. A lower price may signal that there is something hidden that other people know about and you don't – hence as a buyer you are more likely to stay out or to sell. A consequence of this is that credit markets can dry up – and this is indeed what interbank markets do at times. For this reason, it is naïve to expect that the problem of bank runs may have an exclusively private solution.

An efficient provision of LOLR has to be consistent and credible – so as to steer expectations and prevent the runs that it is supposed to address, which is the best possible world. However, it should not be taken for granted to the extent that it stokes moral hazard – the expectation by bank management that, whatever risks they take, they will always be eventually bailed out by the central bank.[29]

A new question: LROR for non-banks and governments

The attentive reader will have already figured out that the Diamond-Dybvig logic that we saw on page 79 applies to any agent or institution who holds short-term liabilities, subject to rollover risk, and illiquid assets, which can only be sold at a cost.

One actor that shares a lot of similarity with banks, at least from this standpoint, is the government. Its debt is made of liquid instruments and, depending on its average maturity, it may be subject to rollover risk in the same way as banks. (Rollover risk is the risk that creditors will not buy again the institution's short term debt when it comes due, similar to what happens in a bank run.) Its assets are the most illiquid of all, made of current and future taxes. As a consequence, the government bond market may be characterised by instability and self-fulfilling equilibria.[30] A lender of last resort (LROR) function for central banks to governments would imply, for example, setting a cap on the interest rate by the government to prevent bad equilibria arising from rollover risk.[31] Note that this is conceptually different from the possibility that the central bank monetises debt, which has to do with the government's solvency and the prospect of reducing the real value of debt through inflation. However, from a practical standpoint, and again in the same way as for banks, it may not be easy to distinguish LOLR intervention aimed at preventing self-fulfilling equilibria in the government bond market from outright debt monetisation, and there will always be the suspicion that the former implies the latter down the road.

Another important discussion is whether the LOLR should be extended to financial intermediaries that are not banks, but that nevertheless behave as banks (have fixed liabilities and risky assets), the so-called 'shadow banks' (for example, investment banks). In the global financial crisis, the absence of a LOLR function to shadow banks was one of the main problems that needed to be addressed. On the other hand, shadow banks are less regulated and supervised than banks, which implies that assessing their solvency may be more problematic and so would be separating insolvency from illiquidity.

Debt deflation

Beyond the LOLR function, another important element that is relevant for central banks is the fact that their control of inflation may influence financial stability. The most important channel here is 'debt deflation' – a mechanism originally identified by Irving

Fisher in 1933, the same Irving Fisher of the Fisher equation encountered in Chapter 2 (and a man of many interests, as he was also a strong advocate of vegetarianism).

Debt deflation is a direct consequence of the fact that debt contracts are typically specified in nominal terms, as we have seen. Therefore, a surprise fall in inflation or outright deflation tends to increase the real value of debt for borrowers – up to a point where the real value of debt is unsustainable, and defaults may ensue. For example, suppose that I have debt for 100 euro and deflation strikes, reducing the consumer price index by 10%. This will increase my real debt burden to 110 euro. This mechanism was at play in several episodes of financial crisis, notably in the Great Depression but also – in its open economy version – in the Asian financial crisis at the end of the 1990s.

The existence of debt deflation is another reason why it is important to keep inflation stable and prevent deflation in particular. Borrowers may be the weakest link in societies – after all only they (not creditors) can default and create financial stability, and they are often also the agents in the economy with the highest propensity to consume. Surprise deflation, if not accompanied by default on debt contracts, reduces borrowers' net worth, and may have a disproportionate downward impact on consumption and spending, aggravating a recession.

The financial accelerator

There is yet another transmission channel, also related to financial factors that central banks need to be aware of. It is the 'financial accelerator' channel based on pioneering work by Ben Bernanke, Mark Gertler at New York University and Simon Gilchrist at Boston University.[32]

The details of the model are complicated but its intuition simple: firms face external financing constraints, due to asymmetric information, in particular they can borrow at cheaper terms if they have high net worth. Higher net worth (being richer, in practice) means having 'more skin in the game' when undertaking an investment project – losing more in case of default and bankruptcy. The lender knows this and expects more effort and higher probability of success in case of more skin in the game. Therefore, it also lends at easier terms, e.g. the spread between corporate lending rates and a risk free rate declines.

This mechanism is important for central banks, because it amplifies the effect of their policies due to a financial channel. A rise in the short-term interest rate, for example, may lead to a decline of asset valuations and economic activity, lowering firms' net worth. The fall in net worth makes external financing conditions more costly, credit spreads soar, which in turn further reduces net worth, in a vicious loop.

Bubbles, bubbles

Perhaps the most important aspect of financial stability, not only for central banks but for economic policy more generally, is the risk of unsustainable booms and subsequent busts in credit and asset prices – in short, the ever-present possibility of a 'Minsky moment' which we opened this chapter with. There is a lot of evidence that this is a systematic and recurrent pattern in economic history, which was recently popularised by the excellent book by Carmen Reinhart and Ken Rogoff, *This Time is Different: Eight Centuries of Financial Folly*.[33] Recent research based on over 100 years of data for a group of advanced countries has revealed that financial crises are best predicted by strong credit and house price growth – the so-called 'leveraged bubbles'.[34] At the same time, a policy-maker can never be sure that fast growth of credit and house prices is a harbinger of a crisis to come: there are also 'good' credit booms that should not be stopped, just to complicate matters further.[35]

To illustrate how stability concerns may become a real and substantial drag on the central bank, Markus Brunnermeier at Princeton University and Yuliy Sannikov at Stanford University developed a theory dubbed as 'the I theory of money'.[36] The idea is that the health of financial intermediation and the distribution of resources between debtors and creditors determine inside money creation and the price of risk in the economy. Because of this special role, the financial sector can 'corner' the central bank and force it to run policy so as to support the financial sector – the alternative would be a financial crisis which would also impinge on price stability. The reasoning is in fact familiar: it is to a large extent the same logic as we have seen in Chapter 3 for fiscal dominance. Under financial dominance, it is the real debt of the financial sector that may run out of control, and bring down the economy with it, if the central bank follows a too strict inflation targeting rule.

In the bad state of the world (say, a crisis), monetary policy is forced to 'redistribute' from creditors to debtors, because debtors are the most vulnerable and crucial for the recovery, including for the recovery of inflation. In this view, price and financial stability are largely the same.

Does financial stability matter for monetary policy more broadly?

More generally, taking all we have said into account, what should monetary policy change if financial stability is important – possibly more important than price stability?

The central bank can essentially do two things.[37] First, it could continue to aim at price stability only, and leave financial stability to other policy makers – notably those in charge of macro-prudential policy – namely, policy actions that directly address credit growth and leverage in the financial system, such as caps on loan to value ratios or higher capital requirements for banks. This can be characterised as the mainstream response by most central banks.

Second, they could 'lean against the wind': namely incorporate, in their interest rate policy, the objective of preventing the formation of bubbles in credit and asset prices. This may imply extending the Taylor rule (where interest rates respond to the output gap and inflation only) to include terms related to credit provision, such as credit growth or credit spreads (the spread between interest rates on bank loans and risk free rates).[38] The central bank has to choose the optimal point along a trade-off between attaining price stability and minimising the probability of having a financial crisis – monetary policy becomes a (difficult) balancing act.

An extreme case of this policy is that the central bank should, first, recognise if there is a bubble in, say, housing markets and, second, try to prick the bubble with its interest rate policy. If followed, this is a conduct of monetary policy that, like the LOLR, definitely requires an IQ well above 100!

Leaning against the wind looks like a good common sense proposal, but its implementation may be problematic. A critic of the idea of 'leaning against the wind' is Lars Svensson.[39] He argues that, in realistic calibrations of the economy in standard models, the costs of leaning against the wind clearly exceed the benefits. This is because the empirical estimates of the effects of changes in interest rates on the probability of experiencing a crisis are so small that using interest rates for that objective would create a lot of unnecessary volatility in the economy. Moreover, higher interest rates to reduce the probability of an asset price bubble can even have perverse effects, notably by the debt deflation channel (higher interest rates lead to lower than expected inflation, implying a higher real debt burden for borrowers and more, not less financial fragility). An attempt by the Sveriges Riksbank, Sweden's central bank, to use interest rates for 'leaning against the wind' did not prove durable, and interest rates had to be hastily lowered again.

First, do no harm

Another important consideration in this context is a version of the Hippocratic Oath 'First do no harm' applied in a central banking context: the monetary authority should in any case not create a bubble with its policy, for example by keeping interest rates low for too long. This is a possible concern now in particular, as central banks have been keeping not only short-term, but also long-term rates at very low levels for a long time.

Low interest rates may jeopardise financial stability in a number of ways. First, low interest rates may increase the demand for credit and, by lowering the discount factor, push up asset prices. While this is the normal process whereby monetary policy is transmitted to the economy, it may lead to over-extended balance sheets and borrowers taking on too much risk. Second, low interest rates may stimulate risk taking by the private sector – most notably by financial intermediaries. This is the so-called 'risk taking channel' of monetary policy. The main element of this transmission channel is that low interest rates make households and firms more risk loving, and start a bubble in credit and asset prices – in short, set in motion the upward phase of the Minsky cycle.

There is substantial empirical evidence for this factor, for example from micro data on loans,[40] but we still lack a coherent theory of why there should be a systematic link between interest rates and risk taking. One conjecture is that low interest rates push investors to take on more risk in order to target higher returns compared with some type of benchmark – although also in this case it is not clear how much this is part of the normal transmission channel of monetary policy, and how much is pathological. Moreover, claims that low interest rates cause bubbles and financial stability have to be tempered by the 'Svensson critique', namely by the fact that the association between interest rates and subsequent crises is weak in the macroeconomic data.

Bernanke vs. Taylor

Perhaps the clearest characterisation of this debate can be grasped by looking at the exchange between John Taylor and Ben Bernanke concerning the role of the Federal Reserve in the wake of the global financial crisis. Taylor argues that the deviation of Federal Reserve policy from the Taylor rule in the early 2000s more or less caused the housing bubble and hence the global financial crisis thereafter.[41] He labels that as the 'Great Deviation' coming after the Great Moderation, and pleads for a return to more rule-based policy-making ('getting back on track').

Bernanke counters that monetary policy cannot be run on an autopilot – the Taylor rule is at best a broad guideline for policy, and policy makers know a lot more about the economy than the variables and the parameters of the Taylor rule. More to the point, he provides many elements that suggest that higher leverage and risk taking in the early 2000s (before the global financial crisis) was not a collateral product of monetary policy and the low level of interest rates prevailing then. He underpins his view with two findings. First, in most models the variation in interest rates seen in the early 2000s was just not enough to cause a boom in house prices, and other factors such as regulatory standards are likely to be more important. Second, from a cross country perspective, countries with lower interest rates did not, on average, experience more housing booms. In this view, the Fed indeed did no harm.[42]

Notes

1 I do not want to give the impression here that there is a consensus that the financial cycle exists as a separate phenomenon from other economic shocks. I am myself still not fully convinced of this. An institution that has been very vocal for the existence and importance of a financial cycle is the Bank for International Settlements, which is in a way the central bank of central banks and is an authoritative voice in central banking circles.
2 Rancière, R., Tornell, A. and F. Westermann, 'Systemic Crises and Growth', *Quarterly Journal of Economics* 123, 1, 2008, 359–406.
3 See Mishkin, F., 'Globalization: A Force for Good?', 12 October 2006, at https://www.federalreserve.gov/newsevents/speech/mishkin20061012a.htm.
4 Incidentally, for that reason to my knowledge no consumption credit is ever given through equity, it is always debt. Housing loans are also always debt contracts.
5 Townsend, R., 'Optimal Contracts and Competitive Markets with Costly State Verification', *Journal of Economic Theory* 21, 2, 1979, 265–293.
6 Jovanic, B. and M. Ueda, 'Contracts and Money', *Journal of Political Economy* 105, 4, 1997, 700–708.
7 Alfaro, L. and F. Kanczuk, 'Nominal versus Indexed Debt: A Quantitative Horse Race', *Journal of International Money and Finance* 29, 2010, 1706–1726.
8 Allen, F. and D. Gale, 'Optimal Financial Crises', *Journal of Finance* 53, 1998, 1245–1284.
9 Berger, A. N. and C. Bouwman, 'Bank Liquidity Creation', *Review of Financial Studies* 22, 9, 2009, 3779–3837.

10 See Clerc, L., Derviz, A., Mendicino, C., Moyen, S., Nikolov, K., Stracca, L., Suarez, J. and A. P. Vardoulakis, 'Capital Regulation in a Macroeconomic Model with Three Layers of Default', *International Journal of Central Banking*, June, 2015, 9–63.
11 Diamond, D. and P. Dybvig, 'Bank Runs, Deposit Insurance, and Liquidity', *Journal of Political Economy* 91, 3, 1983, 401–19.
12 Friedman, M. and A. Schwarz, *A Monetary History of the United States*, Princeton University Press, 1963.
13 Romer, C. D., 'The Nation in Depression', *Journal of Economic Perspectives* 7, 2, 1993, 19–39.
14 Friedman and Schwartz (op. cit.).
15 Eichengreen, B. and J. Sachs, 'Exchange Rates and Recovery in the 1930s', *Journal of Economic History* 44, 1984, 925–946.
16 See 'The Great Depression', Federal Reserve History, available at https://www.federalreservehistory.org/essays/great_depression.
17 See Eichengreen, B., *Golden Fetters*, New York: Oxford University Press, 1992; on Eugene Meyer himself, see James Butkiewicz, L., 'Eugene Meyer and the German Influence on the Origin of U.S. Federal Financial Rescues', University of Delaware Working Paper 2013–09, 2013.
18 Almunia, M., Bénétrix, A., Eichengreen, B., O'Rourke, K. and G. Rua, 'From Great Depression to Great Credit Crisis: Similarities, Differences and Lessons', *Economic Policy* 25, 2010, 219–265.
19 See Perri's comments to Almunia et al. (2010).
20 As already noted in Chapter 4, when interest rates are at the zero bound, we normally do not experience a rise in interest rates after a fiscal expansion, which in normal conditions crowds out private investment and reduces the expansionary effect of the policy.
21 In the United States deposit insurance was introduced with the Glass-Steagall Act of 1933, which also created the Federal Deposit Insurance Corporation, or FDIC. Other countries introduced similar legislation at the time or in subsequent years. At the time of writing, all EU countries fully ensure bank deposits up to EUR 100,000 per deposit.
22 See Tucker, P., 'The Lender of Last Resort and Modern Central Banking: Principles and Reconstruction', BIS Papers No 79, 2014. For a good survey of the literature on LOLR see Grossman, R. S. and H. Rockoff, 'Fighting the Last War: Economists on the Lender of Last Resort', NBER Working Paper 20832, 2015.
23 See W. Buiter, 'The Central Bank as Market Maker of Last Resort', 12 August 2007, http://maverecon.blogspot.de/2007/08/central-bank-as-market-maker-of-last.html.
24 See U. Bindseil, *Monetary Policy Implementation*, Oxford: Oxford University Press, 2005; Bordo, M., 'The Lender of Last Resort: Alternative Views and Historical Experience', *Federal Reserve Bank of Richmond Economic Review*, January/February, 1990, 18–29.
25 For a criticism of collateral frameworks see K. G. Nyborg, *Collateral Frameworks: The Open Secret of Central Banks*, Cambridge: Cambridge University Press, 2016; see Bindseil, U. and L. Laeven, 'Confusion about the Lender of Last Resort', 13 January 2017, for a rebuttal, available at http://voxeu.org/article/confusion-about-lender-last-resort. Among other things, they note that central banks have implemented LOLR on a very large scale during and after the global financial crisis and yet have not lost any money doing it, which proves the robustness of their framework. More generally, it is notable that historically the LOLR function is very rarely associated with losses for the provider of this type of lending, both at domestic and international level. Part of the reason is surely that, *de iure* or *de facto*, many LOLR loans are senior to other claims.
26 Goodhart, C. A. E., 'The Changing Role of Central Banks', *Financial History Review* 18, 02, 2011, 135–154.
27 Gorton, G., 'Clearinghouses and the Origin of Central Banking in the United States', *Journal of Economic History* 45, 2, 1985, 277–283.
28 Goodfriend, M. and R. G. King, 'Financial Deregulation, Monetary Policy, and Central Banking', *Federal Reserve Bank of Richmond Economic Review*, May/June, 1988, 3–22.
29 There are other interesting issues related to the LOLR function that, for reasons of space, I cannot address. For example, one question is the seniority of LOLR and private

claims in case of bankruptcy of a bank, and what solution is optimal; see Kahn, C. and J. Santos, 'Allocating bank regulatory powers: Lender of last resort, deposit insurance and supervision', *European Economic Review*, 49, 8, 2005, 2107–2136. Rochet and Vives have several papers modelling the provision of LOLR in realistic setting, where the central bank cannot be sure about illiquidity or insolvency and where sunspots play a role; see for example Rochet, J. C. and X. Vives, 'Coordination Failures and the Lender of Last Resort: Was Bagehot Right after All?', *Journal of the European Economic Association* 2, 2004, 1116–1147.

30 See De Grauwe, P., 'The European Central Bank as a Lender of Last Resort', 18 August 2011, at http://voxeu.org/article/european-central-bank-lender-last-resort.

31 See Calvo, G., 'Servicing the Public Debt: The Role of Expectations', *American Economic Review* 78, 4, 1988, 647–61; Corsetti, G. and L. Dedola, 'The Mystery of the Printing Press: Monetary Policy and Self-fulfilling Debt Crises', CEPR Discussion Paper 11089, 2016.

32 See Bernanke, B., Gertler, M. and S. Gilchrist, 'The Financial Accelerator in a Quantitative Business Cycle Framework', in Taylor, J. B. and Woodford, M. eds., *Handbook of Macroeconomics*, vol. 1, Part C, Elsevier, 1999.

33 Reinhart, C. and K. Rogoff, *This Time is Different: Eight Centuries of Financial Folly*, Princeton University Press, 2011.

34 Jordà, O., Schularick, M. and A. M. Taylor, 'Leveraged Bubbles', NBER Working Papers 21486, 2015.

35 Gorton, G. and G. Ordoñez, 'Good Booms, Bad Booms', NBER Working Papers 22008, 2016; Claessens, S., Dell'Ariccia, G., Igan, D., Laeven, L. and H. Tong, 'Credit Booms and Macrofinancial Stability', *Economic Policy*, 2016, 299–357.

36 Brunnermeier, M. K. and Y. Sannikov, 'The I Theory of Money', NBER Working Paper 22533, 2016.

37 See Smets, F., 'Financial Stability and Monetary Policy: How Closely Interlinked?', *International Journal of Central Banking* 10, 2, 2014, 263–299.

38 Woodford, M., 'Financial Intermediation and Macroeconomic Analysis', *Journal of Economic Perspectives* 24, 4, 2010, 21–44.

39 See Svensson, L., 'Cost-benefit Analysis of Leaning against the Wind', NBER Working Paper 21902, 2016.

40 See Delis, M. D., Hasan, I. and N. Mylonidis, 'The Risk Taking Channel of Monetary Policy in the US: Evidence from Corporate Loan Data', *Journal of Money, Credit and Banking* 49, 1, 2017, 187–213.

41 Taylor, J. B., 'Getting Back on Track: Macroeconomic Policy Lessons from the Financial Crisis', *Federal Reserve Bank of St. Louis Review*, May/June, 2010.

42 Bernanke, B., 'Monetary Policy and the Housing Bubble', 3 January 2010, https://www.federalreserve.gov/newsevents/speech/bernanke20100103a.htm.

6

WILL PAPER CURRENCY DISAPPEAR AND WILL THIS BE A PROBLEM?

Paper currency is the primary and most known form of fiat money, so that the two are closely associated in people's imagination. Opponents of fiat money often vent their anger towards a proxy target, paper currency. There is a long list of economists, politicians and thinkers who have expressed their criticism of paper currency. Famously, criticism was particularly high, and is still widely quoted, among the Founders of the United States. For example James Madison thought that 'paper money is unjust' and Alexander Hamilton, the legendary first Treasury secretary, warned that:

> To emit an unfunded paper as the sign of value ought not to continue a formal part of the Constitution, nor ever hereafter to be employed; being, in its nature, pregnant with abuses, and liable to be made the engine of imposition and fraud; holding out temptations equally pernicious to the integrity of government and to the morals of the people.[1]

At least, for much of history the issuance of banknotes was backed by gold or silver, though not consistently and with suspensions. Since 1971, however, paper currency and gold are no longer connected at all; paper currency stands or falls on its own.

In this chapter we are going to focus on paper currency in its physical characteristics, not on the broader question of fiat currency vs. commodity based monies. The question we will be focusing on is whether paper currency is a good technology to underpin fiat money and what could happen in the case of its demise.

But who invented paper currency? For that, we need to turn to the Far East.

According to most accounts, the first to use paper notes as forms of money were the Chinese during the Song dynasty in the 11th century – which in turns reflects the fact that paper more generally is a Chinese invention, dating back to centuries before Christ. The Venetian traveller Marco Polo (1254–1324) was among the very first to note the use of paper currency in China. Soon thereafter, paper notes started to circulate in Europe as well, first occasionally and then more widely especially from the 17th century, starting from the letters of exchange that we saw in Chapter 1. Ironically, China was also the first country to largely ban paper currency in the 15th century during the Ming dynasty, and did not resume its use in a wide manner until the 20th century. During that period, China had a monetary system predominantly based on silver.

A primer on e-money and virtual currencies

There is often some confusion on the different concepts and definitions of money, such as e-money and digital or virtual currencies. It is therefore useful to give some definitions first.

E-money is a way to store paper currency electronically. Typically, it is embodied in a magnetic card, such as the Octopus card widely used in Hong Kong, initially designed to pay for transportation and later used for a wide range of payments. The substitution between paper currency and e-money therefore does not change the overall demand for outside money, but it does reduce the role of paper currency. Some forms of e-money however are more a substitution between electronic purses and inside money such as bank deposits, and therefore they are immaterial for the role of paper currency.

Other forms of so-called 'plastic money', such as debit and credit cards, or online services such as Paypal, or apps like Google Wallet,[2] are essentially ways to mobilise bank deposits via electronic or magnetic means. They make it easier to make transfers of deposits between one bank and another. To the extent that they replace paper currency, they represent a shift from outside to inside money. I don't need cash for my transactions if I can use plastic money.

Virtual or digital currencies are another matter altogether. They are an alternative form of outside money, with a floating exchange rate with government-backed fiat money. A virtual currency such as Bitcoin is as different from the euro as it is, say, the US dollar – actually the difference is perhaps even larger. In the final chapter we will see whether digital currencies may represent a form of currency competition which may eventually undermine the monopolistic role of central banks. In sum, e-money and plastic money are redeemable in fiat (paper) money; digital currencies are not.

Preferences for paper or plastic money are shaped by culture and norms, in a way that is not always easy to explain. Generally speaking, paper currency is still very popular in Europe and Japan, while it plays much less of a role in the United States. A trip from the United States to Europe can be a shocking experience from a monetary point of view. It is possible, speaking by personal experience, to travel in the US for weeks without holding a single paper dollar, but try that in Europe at your peril. In emerging countries acceptance of plastic money is unpredictable;

I have seen acceptance of credit cards in unexpected and remote places. In China, the social messaging app WeChat is also widely used for payments (unlike its Western counterpart WhatsApp), but for a taxi ride from Shanghai airport, China's most developed city, you need paper renminbi no matter what.

It is reasonable to ask ourselves whether currency will eventually disappear, in the wake of technological innovation in payments that is clearly visible in many parts of the world. The important questions are three: Would we want this to happen? Is it happening? And would it matter for monetary policy? We will address each of these questions in turn.

Should we ditch paper currency?

Paper currency can legitimately be seen as archaic, at least if we do not consider how high tech current banknotes may be nowadays in order to prevent counterfeiting. The fact that something was considered to be useful in 17th century Europe does not imply that we should continue to use it in the 21st century. And paper currency does have some important disadvantages, which are well explained for example in Ken Rogoff's book *The Curse of Cash*.[3]

Of course, the biggest downside of paper currency is the zero lower bound on the nominal interest rate. No paper currency, no zero bound, and no need to do Quantitative Easing, forward guidance and other non-standard monetary policies, with all their potential side effects. Without paper currency, central banks could run monetary policy on an autopilot, following the Taylor rule. This is by far the most important reason why thinking about abolishing paper currency makes sense.

Another important disadvantage of paper currency is that it facilitates illegal activities. Paper currency is anonymous and perfectly (if of course unwillingly) designed for illegal activities, and in fact large denomination banknotes are often used mainly for that purpose. I have personally never seen a 500 euro banknote, but according to the available statistics this banknote represents a large portion, in value terms, of the stock of currency in circulation in the euro area; presumably, it is widely held by agents with whom I do not frequency interact, and probably you do not either.[4] Ken Rogoff has proposed that eliminating high denomination banknotes would also go a long way towards removing the zero lower bound, because it would raise the cost of storing large values in cash.[5]

Third, counterfeiting is still a significant problem, despite large technological advances by issuers. Counterfeiting is as old as money, of course, and even governments and kings have engaged in counterfeiting. Philip IV 'the Fair' of France, for example, is even mentioned in Dante Alighieri's *La Divina Commedia* as a counterfeiter. One could see counterfeiting as a form of spontaneous money creation, but it is certainly a very rudimentary and sub-optimal form of 'monetary policy'.[6]

Finally, cash is inconvenient as a form of payment and can cause, for example, queues at supermarkets and shops.

However, before we rush to ditch paper currency we should also consider a few of its important advantages. Some of them are indeed the flip side of the cons.

Start with the zero lower bound. The argument can be made that precisely the fact that no negative interest rate can be written on paper currency protects savers from the vagaries of fiat money. As we know, there is no limit to the issuance of fiat money and citizens may feel at the mercy of the government is the latter is able to impose any (negative) interest rate on the now entirely electronic fiat money. For example, Lars Feld, a German economist at the University of Freiburg, has been reported to say that paper currency is 'minted freedom'.[7] A related concern is that an entirely electronic form of money would make it easier for governments to tax citizens; no more trips to offshore financial centres with bags loaded with cash. Paper currency, in the same way as offshore financial centres, may be one way to escape from rapacious governments and possibly discipline them. Whether this is considered to be desirable depends to a large extent on whether governments are seen as forces of good or of evil.

For similar reasons, anonymity can also be seen as an upside. We have already relinquished a lot of privacy, the argument goes, should we really go the full way and be monitored in all we do and pay by, say, Facebook or Google, not to speak of the government or the Secret Service? Although paper currency may be inconvenient, especially for large transactions, there is a (perhaps niche) market for it that will continue to exist in contexts where anonymity is valued, which may go beyond the perimeter of illegal activities (and some illegal activities may be morally sound, for example when prohibited by a tyrannical government). After all, paper books continue to exist despite all the electronic competition, and according to some they are even experiencing a revival.[8] On the other hand, it is not clear how much people are really attached to privacy, especially when it costs money.[9]

These considerations suggest that it may be premature to announce the death of paper currency. Moreover, it is important to keep in mind that any transition to an entirely electronic currency would have to be introduced in the main advanced countries simultaneously, at least if it is a result of a policy decision. A government-imposed restriction on the use of paper currency would encourage the use of alternative paper currencies, if there is a residual demand for it that the policy suppresses. Engineering a global phasing out of paper currency may be problematic, due to heterogeneity in preferences in different countries.

But is it happening?

After all is said and done, can we say that paper currency is declining at least, remorselessly hunted by technological innovation? The evidence for that is not that clear, in fact.

Figure 6.1 shows currency in circulation as a share of Gross Domestic Product (a measure of economic activity) in the world's four largest economies, i.e. the United States, China, Japan and the euro area. The figure documents the heterogeneity in the levels, reflecting cultural differences in the use of cash in transactions referred to earlier. In Germany, for example, a common view is that cash allows for a better real time tracking of current spending. There is a German expression that

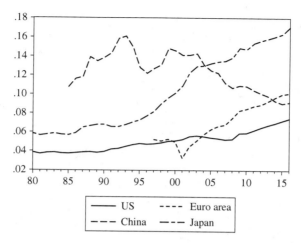

FIGURE 6.1 Currency in circulation as a share of Gross Domestic Product in the world's four largest economies.
Source: IMF International Financial Statistics and World Economic Outlook.

says '*Nur Bares ist Wahres*' (only cash is real). It may also be related to another factor, namely the aversion to debt, which is epitomised by the fact that 'debt' and 'guilt' are captured by the same word in German ('*Schuld*').

Beyond country differences, it is notable that there is no clear downward trend in the data for currency in circulation. The only country where paper currency appears to be on a secular decline, as a share of Gross Domestic Product, is China, probably due to the strong economic growth rather than to a contraction of cash as such.

One qualification to be made here is that a lot of cash is held and used abroad, and we don't know very well how to measure it. This is particularly the case for the US dollar, for which perhaps 50% circulate outside the United States, and also for the euro especially in Eastern Europe.[10] However, there is no particular reason to believe that foreign use is distorting the estimate of the trends, although it is certainly material for estimating the levels. As far as we know, there is no sign of cash disappearing; we remain awash in cash.

A fall in seignorage?

Central banks make profits from the issuance of cash, often a lot of them. The reason for that is simple: paper currency, a liability for the central bank, carries zero nominal interest rate; central bank assets normally yield a positive nominal interest rate, even if they are risk free (e.g., government bonds). Moreover, the production costs are normally only a small fraction of the value of the central bank liabilities; in the case of bank reserves, which are electronic, the cost is practically zero.

The difference between the rate of return on assets and the funding cost (close to zero) is the premium paid by holders of central bank money due to the liquidity services provided by it, in a situation of relative scarcity.[11] Central bank profits, called in a quite archaic way 'seignorage' (from a French word indicating the right of the lord, 'seigneur', to mint money), are larger, *ceteris paribus*, if interest rates are higher and if the central bank balance sheet is large. When central banks undertake non-standard policies such as Quantitative Easing, interest rates are low or close to zero, which is bad for profits, but the central bank balance sheet is large, which keeps seignorage high. Can the central bank extract profits without limits from its monopoly rights to issue money? Clearly not, because, like every monopolist, it is eventually constrained by a demand function, and in this case the relevant demand function is money demand, more precisely the demand for outside money as opposed to other short-term assets. (It is the same principle that is valid for any monopolist. For example, a monopolist of, say, tobacco cannot set too high prices, lest it pushes consumers towards other goods entirely.) If the central bank issues a lot of outside money to cash in more seignorage, eventually it will lead to inflation, which acts as a tax on money; the public will eventually economise on money, in turn leading to a fall in seignorage. The seignorage-maximising level of outside money lies therefore at some level between zero and very large values.[12]

Profit seeking was paramount in the early stage of central banking, for example at the time of the creation of the Bank of England in the late 17th century, but nowadays central banks pass seignorage back to governments, which is morally sound (and consistent with their valued independence) because they derive their monopoly rights from State laws. Of course, they subtract something for their operating expenses and for building up buffers against risks, and they have some latitude on that, which is of course a manifestation of the financial independence of central banks – indeed, as we have already seen, they would not be really independent if they were on a tight leash from the government on expenses.[13]

How large is seignorage, really? It varies a lot by country and in time, but it is typically a small but non-negligible share of government revenues. In the United States, where seignorage is lower than elsewhere because of the smaller role of cash in transactions compared with other advanced countries, seignorage still accounts for between 1% and 2% of Gross Domestic Product (GDP).

A decline in the use of paper currency, and in favour of other forms of money, everything else being equal, clearly erodes seignorage. Moreover, the increasing tendency to pay interests on reserves (see Chapter 3) is another factor that may contribute to an erosion of central bank profits. This would be a first relevant downside of a shift away from paper currency, at least for governments who would lose a cheap source of financing. On the other hand, from a welfare point of view it would represent the removal or reduction of a rent induced by monopoly rights, so it may not necessarily be a welfare loss for citizens.

A challenge for monetary control?

Relevant as seignorage may be, the bigger question related to the disappearance of paper currency is the challenge it might pose for monetary control. As we saw in Chapter 2, in textbook models central bank control of the interest rate and inflation entirely depends on the LM curve, i.e. on the demand for paper currency and bank reserves (in fact, more the latter). If the LM curve becomes more price sensitive, implying that households and firms hold currency and bank reserves only in small proportion and only if the opportunity cost is very low, it may become more problematic to manipulate the supply of outside money to achieve a given interest rate objective. This is indeed the view of some economists, see for example the debate between Benjamin Friedman (Harvard University) and Charles Goodhart (London School of Economics), who wondered whether central banks 'can survive the IT revolution'.[14]

The main concern related to monetary control is that the LM curve (the demand for outside money) could become infinitely price sensitive (that is, it reacts a lot to minor changes in the interest rate), in practice implying that the public would *not* hold *any* central bank money unless it has exactly the same interest rate as other short-term safe instruments such as bank deposits and Treasury bills. If that is the case, outside money and short-term debt become perfect substitutes, and controlling the short-term interest rate can only be achieved by taking positions in that market, which is very large in most advanced countries. In other words, central banks would have to 'lean against the market' and take very large net positions in the market for all short-term securities in order to affect the interest rate. This would be both more difficult operationally and riskier, and would change the nature of monetary policy in a fundamental way.

Note that this view needs to be qualified by the reality that the only portion of outside money that matters for monetary policy implementation is bank reserves, which are already electronic. The concern about the disappearance of paper currency for monetary control is therefore an indirect one, based on the possibility that lower demand for paper currency also reduces the need for banks to hold reserves. At least in part, this may be reasonable to expect, because banks mainly hold reserves to face sudden withdrawals of cash from their deposits, or are asked to do so by reserve requirements based on the same underlying reason.

The cashless limit

The opposite and more optimistic view is that central banks do not need to lean against the market to control the short-term interest rate. As long as central banks' liabilities *define* the economy's unit of account, central banks will always be able to influence their price. This is the view commonly known as the 'cashless limit' and associated with Michael Woodford's work.[15] Analytically, it shows that the central bank is in control of the short-term interest rate even if the LM curve (recall, the demand for central bank money) converges to the cashless limit, i.e. to being infinitely price elastic. In this view, there is no need to carry out very large net operations to control the interest rate.

Beyond the specific modelling assumptions in Woodford's work the fundamental reason why this is the case is that there is no 'natural' level of the *nominal* interest rate against which the central bank has to lean. In other words, in a purely private market the level of the nominal short-term interest rate is essentially indeterminate. Surely, the real interest rate may be pinned down by fundamentals, such as the rate of time preference or technological changes, but nothing apart from the central bank pins down the nominal rate.[16] Therefore, a gentle push by the central bank in either direction would allow it to control the level, without the need (at least, most of the time) to carry out large transactions. This, in turn, is consistent with what we have seen in Chapter 3: central banks appear to determine the level of interest rates directly, mostly through the corridor system, without the need to enforce the level through large open market operations. Overall, it is fair to say that a majority of economists now support Woodford's view on the fact that the disappearance of paper currency does not pose a material risk for monetary control, although specific aspects of the 'cashless limit' model have been criticised.[17]

A broader conclusion which is worth emphasising here is that this shows that outside money is much more than paper currency. Banknotes are the physical manifestation of outside money, the 'portable tokens' that we saw in the first chapter of this book, but the concept of outside money goes well beyond it. The main characteristic of outside money is that only that form of money, which nowadays is made of central bank liabilities, is 'full money', whereas all other instruments are only 'quasi money', which are redeemable to a larger or smaller degree in outside money. The role of outside money in the economy, and its possible disappearance, is therefore not a question of technological development but a social and political issue, on which technology has only a very indirect and possibly insignificant impact. If this is true, it is quite possible that central banks will continue to 'rule the roost'.[18]

In conclusion, paper currency is not disappearing, which will continue to pose the problems of the zero lower bound on interest rates and of illegal transactions, but even if it would really disappear, on its own this fact should not cause major distress for central banks or challenges to monetary control, although it would most probably lead to a fall in seigniorage. Everything considered, central banks would probably benefit from the disappearance of paper currency, because it would eliminate the ZLB problem.

India's great demonetisation experiment

If one wanted to design a natural experiment to see what happens when eliminating paper currency from circulation, probably India's demonetisation of 2016 would come closest. What do we learn from this experience?

In November 2016, India's government, led by Narendra Modi, made an intervention that is remarkably rare in monetary history, although not wholly unprecedented for India (something similar had already been done in 1946, in order to punish 'black capitalists'). The government decided to take high denomination banknotes out of circulation, with the objective of reducing corruption and other illegal activities, as well as symbolizing a new order. Citizens were asked to return 500- and 1000-rupee banknotes (86% of the value of all currency in circulation) to banks by the end of December, where they would be converted into new banknotes if they were found to be 'legitimate'. It is now widely referred to as India's 'great demonetisation experiment'. How did it go?

The effect on economic activity was visible, but probably not large. The official data point to steady real GDP growth at the end of 2016, and therefore suggest that the impact of the great demonetisation may have been small from a macroeconomic perspective. Moreover, there has been no report of any problem by the Reserve Bank of India concerning monetary control – namely, control of interest rates and of the monetary policy stance. However, the quality of the data is not to be taken for granted and there have been widespread reports of inconvenience and hardship around the country. The main problem of India's experiment was its speed – even advocates of the elimination of currency like Ken Rogoff agree that any transition out of cash should be done slowly and gradually.[19]

But if it wasn't necessarily an economic victory, it was certainly a political success: soon after the demonetisation Modi's party won by a landslide in the elections in Uttar Pradesh. Maybe the Indians did not love their old rupees all that much.

Notes

1 Holloway, C. and B. P. Wilson, *The Political Writings of Alexander Hamilton*, Cambridge University Press, Volume 1, 2017.
2 Google Wallet is a way to use your credit card using the mobile phone. The use of the mobile phone for retail payments is projected to rise, in particular in emerging countries.
3 Rogoff, K., *The Curse of Cash*, Princeton University Press, 2016.
4 As of May 2016, the European Central Bank decided to phase out the 500 euro banknote.
5 Rogoff (op. cit.).
6 Of course, this consideration has to be counterbalanced by the risk of cybercrime for electronic forms of money, which are potentially even more harmful and uncontrolled.
7 See https://www.zerohedge.com/news/2017-02-01/alternative-fact-cashless-society.
8 See for example https://www.theguardian.com/books/2017/mar/14/ebook-sales-continue-to-fall-nielsen-survey-uk-book-sales.
9 See Athey, S., Catalini, C. and C. Tucker, 'The Digital Privacy Paradox: Small Money, Small Costs, Small Talk', NBER Working Paper No. 23488, 2017.
10 See European Central Bank, 'The Use of Euro Banknotes – Results of Two Surveys among Households and Firms', *Monthly Bulletin*, April, 2011.
11 As noted, in a liquidity trap when the interest rate is at the zero bound, the public is satiated with central bank money, and money and other short-term securities are perfect substitutes.
12 It would be interesting to see if an optimal policy, from a societal welfare point of view, can be designed to be the one that maximises central bank profits, so it is the strategy that a profit maximising central bank would pursue. I am not aware of any systematic study of this question.
13 At the same time, they need to show restraint in their operating expenses, in order not to lose credibility and trust with the general public.
14 See Friedman, B. M., 'The Future of Monetary Policy: The Central Bank as an Army with Only a Signal Corps?', *International Finance* 2, 1999, 321–338; Goodhart, C. A. E., 'Can Central Banking Survive the IT Revolution?', *International Finance* 3, 2, 2000, 189–209. A good overview is in McCallum, B. T., 'Monetary Policy in Economies with Little or No Money', NBER Working Paper 9838, 2003.

15 Woodford, M., 'Monetary Policy in a World without Money', *International Finance* 3, 2, 2000, 229–260.
16 Note that we are abstracting from open economy considerations. In open economy and in the presence of a fixed exchange rate arrangement the interest rate is pinned down by the need to maintain the peg, and has to track the interest rate of the base currency.
17 See Rogers, C., 'Doing Without Money: A Critical Assessment of Woodford's Analysis', mimeo, 2004.
18 Sardoni, C., 'Why Central Banks (and Money) Rule the Roost', Working Paper no. 457, The Levy Economics Institute of Bard College, 2006.
19 Rogoff (op. cit.).

7

WILL WE EVER HAVE A GLOBAL CENTRAL BANK?

So far, our focus has been domestic – we have seen the central bank as an essentially domestic matter. In this chapter, we will turn to the open economy dimension of central banking, which will be illustrated by addressing the question of whether we will ever have a global central bank and a world currency. Currently, central banks are organised along Westphalian lines, namely depending on State borders. The only exception is the monetary unions, the most important of which is, of course, the Economic and Monetary Union in Europe.

During this chapter we will see whether establishing a world currency is a worthwhile long-term objective for the international monetary system. A substantial part, though not all, of the answer to this question hinges on whether flexible exchange rates are desirable or not. It is useful to start from a closed economy context and see what is different in the open economy and what role exchange rates play. We will then see whether establishing a world currency might be advantageous, and under what conditions.

We will compare fixed and flexible exchange rates mainly from two perspectives, namely, (i) how they fare in terms of relative price adjustment at international level and, relatedly, (ii) whether they facilitate the external adjustment of trade (current account) imbalances. At the end, however, we will argue that there are additional important elements in central banks that would also need to be addressed, for example the lender of last resort function.

The international monetary system

It is useful to start from the definition of the international monetary system, which is the international counterpart of a monetary standard in a closed economy. We normally think of the international monetary system as a combination of three elements. First, which currencies are used for international payments (both for trade and financial assets), namely which currencies are 'international currencies'; the system has in fact always been two-tiered, in that there are at most a few internationally used currencies ('reserve currencies') due to economies of scale.[1] Second, the exchange rate regime both between international currencies and between them and the remaining currencies. Third, the adjustment of balance of payments imbalances, in particular for those countries that pay imports in foreign currency and therefore need foreign currency in order to pay for them.[2]

A configuration of the international monetary system can be symmetric or not, meaning that the monetary standard providing the nominal anchor can be a global one or one based on a specific hegemonic country. The Gold Standard is an example of a symmetric standard: gold provides the nominal anchor, and all countries are more or less subject to it. In the post-Bretton Woods regime (which we will turn to in a moment) the system has become largely asymmetric: the US dollar is at the centre of the system and has provided, in particular in the first two decades of Bretton Woods, the world's nominal anchor. Therefore, in this period only the US has experienced a significant degree of monetary policy independence.

Over recent years, financial globalisation has made great strides. The stock and flow of cross-border assets and liabilities now dwarf trade in goods and services, and many important questions around the international monetary system concern trade in assets rather than traditional exports and imports. For example, one important question – which I will not address for reasons of space – is the provision of safe and liquid assets and how the United States and the US dollar, also in this respect, represent a quite unique case.

Note that in a world with perfectly flexible prices and no transaction costs, the choice of which currency to use for international transactions would be largely inconsequential. International trade could be settled in any currency and then converted, at market exchange rates, into any other currency. It is because of sticky prices and other nominal rigidities that the choice of the exchange rate regime – and indeed the international monetary system more broadly – has economic significance.

The Bretton Woods conference

The current international monetary system is still influenced to a significant extent by the arrangement designed in the Bretton Woods conference in 1944, where the soon-to-be victorious powers of World War II met, led by Britain and especially the United States, in order to re-design the international monetary system after the collapse of the Gold Standard and the turbulence in the interwar years.[3]

The main outcome of the conference was to establish a dollar standard system centred on the US dollar. Currencies would be pegged, at least in the short term, to the dollar, which would in turn have a fixed parity against gold.

Moreover, the International Monetary Fund (IMF) was created, a credit union to which countries contribute quota (similar to equity) and whose main task is to lend to countries that are in temporary difficulties in external borrowing and balance of payments imbalances. If a country wanted to borrow, it needed to be monitored (and its policies influenced) by the IMF, in order to prevent moral hazard. It also created an artificial asset, the IMF-sponsored Special Drawing Rights (SDR), which was hoped to be the embryo of a truly global currency – an expectation that so far has been largely disappointed, despite repeated calls to raise its role at the expense of the main international currencies.

An important element of the Bretton Woods agreement, but not of the actual regime, was the fact that exchange rate parities were adjustable for longer-term disequilibria; the system was in fact designed to prevent *short-term* volatility in exchange rates, not medium-term re-alignments. *De facto*, however, European countries and Japan (still reeling from the destruction of World War II) have largely given up on this possibility at least in the first two decades of the Bretton Woods regime, and preferred to 'import' US monetary policy by pegging to the US dollar. Tthe situation would eventually change in the 1960s, when European countries were considerably stronger and US inflation higher.

Concerning the centre country, the United States, the commitment to convert dollars into gold was more pro forma than real. It was not a real constraint until the late 1960s, when doubts about convertibility started being widespread. As a result, at least until the early 1960s the United States enjoyed a large degree of monetary policy independence, which it used wisely to establish low and stable inflation and a very open capital account, which in turn further reinforced the dominant role of the US dollar.

In fact, one enduring element of the Bretton Woods regime, despite its collapse in 1971, is the still central role of the US dollar in the international monetary system – ironically, it has lasted despite a collapse *which was caused by the US dollar itself*. The British delegation at the Bretton Woods conference, led by John Maynard Keynes, had tried to establish an international currency, the Bancor,[4] and a system of adjustment of balance of payments imbalances that would penalise both deficit and surplus countries.[5] In the end, the financial strength of the United States (at the time the largest creditor nation, while Britain was a debtor nation) prevailed and the system was designed around the US dollar and protecting the interests of creditor countries. The current international monetary system runs on dollars, which may be a source of fragility because the US cannot take this into account if this is not aligned with its domestic interests. Therefore, the world economy risks being 'hostage' to the vagaries of US monetary policy based on US domestic developments.

Enduring problems of the Bretton Woods order

Both the 'old' and the 'new' Bretton Woods faced the problem of how to discipline the issuer of the reserve currency, the United States. This problem was noted in particular by Robert Triffin, a Belgian-American economist who was an academic but also served in the Federal Reserve, the IMF and the OECD. The so-called 'Triffin dilemma' stipulates that the international role of the dollar is ultimately incompatible with a well-behaved US economy underpinning that role. Triffin's reasoning was that in order to increase international liquidity, the world needs dollars and dollars can only be provided if the US runs a persistent balance of payments deficit. This, however, may stoke inflation in the US and a depreciation of the dollar over time, undermining at least some of the characteristics that make the US dollar desirable in the first place.

It is now recognised that the Triffin dilemma is not relevant anymore in a world of high capital mobility, because dollars can be created largely independent of a US balance of payments deficit. For example, the US can have large external liabilities, which contribute to international liquidity, but also have an equally large amount of external assets. Gross, rather than net capital flows matter today, unlike in Triffin's times. The Triffin dilemma, however, may be alive in a new incarnation. The United States, as a result of its status as the issuer of the world reserve currency, can borrow very cheaply from foreign investors. This feature has been lambasted as the 'exorbitant privilege' of the US by Valéry Giscard d'Estaing, a former President of France; American politician John Connally (better known for sitting beside President Kennedy and having been seriously wounded at the time of Kennedy's 1963 assassination in Dallas), on his part, defined the US dollar as 'our currency, but your problem'. This capacity for cheap borrowing may encourage the US to borrow too much from abroad, eventually undermining the dollar's position as a stable currency.[6]

Another problem that remains largely unsolved since Bretton Woods is the symmetry in the adjustment of current account imbalances — namely, the fact that having a surplus of exports over imports is seen as unproblematic, whereas having a deficit requires active effort to correct the imbalance. This was well known already to Keynes — who used to call it the 'secular international problem' — and even before him. In fact an asymmetric behaviour was visible already during the Gold Standard: it was always easier to accumulate more gold reserves, but experiencing a deficit or an outflow of reserves was often seen as problematic. This behaviour is, of course, collectively inconsistent and may lead to global deflationary pressure.[7]

At the core, the problem of the asymmetry of the adjustment derives from the fact that it is difficult for the international community to force countries to adjust their trade surpluses, because they are not subject to market discipline in the same way as the deficit countries. If a country runs a deficit for too long and accumulates net foreign liabilities it may sooner or later be forced to adjust by capital outflows — essentially, because no lender would want to continue refinancing it. But there is no particular problem in accumulating net foreign assets indefinitely — if we exclude, of course, the fact that citizens consume less than they potentially could (it is worth recalling here that the only purpose of exports is to be able to buy imports). This is particularly the case if the export sector forms a strong lobby and has an undue influence on the government, whereas importers are more dispersed and weaker politically. Granted, over time a stronger exchange rate should eliminate a trade surplus, and this remains the key adjustment mechanism also for surplus countries, but, as we will soon see, movements in the exchange rate are at best a slow channel in correcting imbalances in either direction.

Exchange rate regimes

It is useful to recall the different exchange rate regimes that are theoretically possible, in particular for the non-reserve currencies (reserve currencies tend to float between themselves). In a floating regime, the country in question is independent in its monetary policy and accepts fluctuations in exchange rates as determined by the market. In a peg, countries sell or buy foreign currencies to appreciate or depreciate the exchange so as to keep it close to a given parity (which may be adjustable). A managed float – which is very common especially in emerging markets – is an intermediate case between the two, implying that some variability in the exchange rate is tolerated, but excessive volatility is not (often in an asymmetric way: appreciation is often more worrying than depreciation). Finally, a 'currency board' is an extreme case of peg, where the central bank keeps foreign exchange reserve equal to the whole amount of outside money in circulation in domestic currency. While this is a very robust arrangement in terms of vulnerability to runs, it is not the same as an irrevocably fixed exchange rate, as it is sometimes argued, because also a currency board can be abandoned, as the experience of Argentina (who had a currency board arrangement with the USD) in the early 2000s clearly shows.[8]

As already hinted, after the collapse of Bretton Woods in the early 1970s the main industrial countries have tended to have freely floating exchange rates between them, with the important exception of European countries who eventually chose to form a monetary union, the euro area. Even among the supposedly freely floating countries, moreover, policy-makers also keep a keen eye on exchange rates. In 1985, for example, the G7 countries agreed to depreciate the US dollar at the Plaza agreement, after the dollar had appreciated very strongly in the wake of high US interest rates during the Volcker dis-inflation. A similar smaller scale intervention was undertaken to support the euro in 2000.

The economics of exchange rates is complex and it is not surprising that countries have struggled to find the best exchange rate arrangement for them, and also that the optimal design of the international monetary system remains an elusive concept. We will now see how difficult it is to evaluate benefits and costs of floating exchange rates.

Exchange rates as a by-product of (relative) monetary policy

A useful starting point is to consider that, in the simplest models at least, the exchange rate is simply a by-product of relative monetary policies, namely the difference between the domestic and the foreign short term interest rate. Consider two economies, say Home and Foreign, and two interest rates R (domestic) and R★ (foreign) and a log nominal exchange rate s, the Uncovered Interest Parity (UIP) holds that:

$$s_t - E_t s_{t+1} = R_t - R_t^*$$

In order to equalise expected (nominal) returns on risk free bonds in the two countries, the expected depreciation of the Home currency must be equal to the interest rate spread between the Home and the Foreign country. In words,

$$\text{expected depreciation} = \text{domestic interest rate} - \text{foreign interest rate}$$

For example, suppose that the short-term interest rate is 2% in the Eurozone and 1% in the US; according to the UIP, this implies the *expectation* of a euro depreciation vs. the dollar by 1%. In other words, low interest rate currencies should tend to appreciate.

Note that this equality holds only with perfect financial integration, namely without capital controls. Also note that this holds *ex ante* and is therefore subject to risk (unlike the Covered Interest Parity, or CIP, where the exchange rate risk is eliminated through hedging). There is somewhat of a puzzle surrounding the UIP. On the one hand, empirical estimates typically fail to confirm it, especially at short horizons, suggesting that risk premia play a major role or that the model is simply mis-specified. At the same time, countries do feel constrained by the UIP, in that policy-makers understand that higher (lower) interest rates are associated with appreciation (depreciation) pressures.

The trilemma

The UIP relation makes it clear that, as is well known since Robert Mundell's work in the early 1960s, interest rates, exchange rates and capital mobility are closely related. In particular, one cannot control domestic interest rates (domestic monetary policy) and foreign exchanges simultaneously and have capital mobility at the same time; one of the three has to go (trilemma). Despite the fact that the UIP has had, to say the least, limited empirical success, the trilemma is often perceived to be a real constraint for central banks and governments, in particular in small open economies and emerging markets.

There is a substantial amount of research on the question of whether a floating exchange rate regime does protect small countries from shifts in the monetary policy of larger countries. In theory, the UIP would firmly say that it does, because it is only under a fixed exchange rate regime and financial integration (no capital controls) that the foreign interest rate determines the domestic interest rate. The empirical evidence is much more controversial. While some papers do find evidence that it is indeed the case,[9] others do not, in particular when they look at the non-systematic part of monetary policy, namely the component of monetary policy that is not explained by domestic fundamentals.[10]

Relative price adjustment in the open economy

Similar to a closed economy, and optimal and welfare-maximising allocation can be defined as one where relative prices are flexible and fully reflect fundamental factors such as preferences and technology. For example, if, say, German cars become more attractive than American cars, it is usually optimal that their relative price rises, adjusting for exchange rate changes. In the international context, we can think of different product varieties produced in different countries, with an elasticity of substitution (namely, how desirable is one product relative to another) between them, which in the international context is called 'Armington elasticity'.[11]

In this context, the relevant question is whether flexible exchange rates make the relative adjustment easier or rather represent a source of unwanted volatility in relative prices. Despite the centrality of this question, there is actually rather limited empirical research speaking to it.

Milton Friedman famously remarked in a book published in 1953 that flexible exchange rates are desirable because they make (sticky) domestic prices more flexible in the open economy.[12] Flexible exchange rates however make international relative prices more flexible only if two conditions hold, namely, (i) exchange rates are passed on to prices (pass-through) and (ii) exchange rates move endogenously (namely, responding to economic trends) and are not themselves an autonomous source of shock (namely, they move for reasons of their own). Both propositions can be challenged, although they are not necessarily wrong in all contexts.

Flexible exchange rates are desirable as conduit of adjustment only for real shocks, not necessarily for nominal shocks. For example, a study has shown that a flexible exchange rate regime helps in the adjustment to terms of trade shocks (shocks that increase the relative price between exports and imports – for example when oil prices increase and the country is an oil exporter).[13] Other studies focus on the adjustment following natural disasters in fixed or flexible exchange rates, finding that the recovery after a disaster is faster under flexible exchange rates.[14] More generally, however, there are not many studies looking at the role of the exchange rate regime conditional on well-defined structural shocks, which is what one should do if this question is to be answered in a rigorous manner.

Exchange rate pass-through

As mentioned, a first pre-condition for flexible exchange rates to contribute to a smoother adjustment of international relative prices is that exchange rate movements are transmitted to domestic prices.

A large body of research suggests that pass-through (transmission) from exchange rates to (retail and wholesale) prices is limited and well below one, even in the long term. This means that, say, a 10% appreciation of the exchange rate results in an increase in, say, the consumer price index of less than 10%, perhaps 5% or so. It is also context-dependent; it is lower in large economies such as the US, but higher, possibly even complete, in emerging economies.[15] One can distinguish, as opposite cases, 'producer currency pricing' (PCP) and 'local currency pricing' (LCP). Under PCP, the law of one price holds. For example, in the previous example German cars become trendier than US cars but prices of cars in domestic currency are sticky. The appreciation of the euro vs. the dollar may make the relative price of German cars more flexible, replicating the desirable flexible price allocation, provided the price of German cars in the US is set in euros (PCP). The euro appreciation switches spending towards US cars, with the result that there is no (unnecessary and excessive) unemployment among US car producers. If the price of a German car is set in dollars in the US (LCP) this desirable adjustment of relative prices does not happen.

Why do firms choose PCP or LCP? Suppose that there is a large depreciation of the domestic currency, say the euro. If German car manufacturers practise LCP they pay salaries in euros, but can sell in US dollars which are now more worthwhile, given the euro depreciation. This increases their profits. Under PCP, they sell in euros and can gain market share. The trade-off faced by firms *ex ante* can thus be defined as one between the stability of their profit margin and the stability of their market share; in principle they will choose PCP vs. LCP depending on the relative benefits of stabilising either, also taking into account that especially large firms can also hedge currency risk, at a cost.

What are the implications of exchange rate pass-through for monetary policy? Under PCP, exchange rates do their job in facilitating international adjustment. It turns out that under PCP the best monetary policy can do in the international context is just to target domestic variables, exactly as it would do in a closed economy context.[16] Flexible exchange rates are desirable under PCP. Under LCP, by contrast, there is no gain from flexible exchange rates, apart possibly from trend depreciation in order to allow for different inflation targets across countries. Also note that the optimality of fixed exchange rates under LCP is not necessarily maintained with more complex models, e.g. those including both traded and non-traded goods. Independent monetary policy may be valuable in that case, e.g. to stabilise the output gap for both types of goods.

An interesting intermediate case is 'dollar pricing', i.e. a mix of PCP and LCP depending on the size of the two countries (say, US and Canada). Under dollar pricing, the US prices both imports and exports in dollars.[17] This is an intermediate case between PCP and LCP, also in terms of monetary policy and desirability of flexible exchange rates.[18]

Exogenous variation in exchange rates?

One important caveat about model-based analysis of exchange rates is that equilibrium models normally do not do a good job at all in explaining, even qualitatively, *actual* exchange rate behaviour. In most models the exchange rate, as noted, is a by-product of relative monetary policies and does not really have a life of its own. This contradicts common sense and the evidence of high volatility of exchange rates, which is difficult to explain based on interest rate differentials alone – there is in fact a large literature on the 'exchange rate disconnect', namely the apparent disconnect of exchange rates from fundamentals. (The intuitive message is that exchange rates appear to have a life of their own!) Most notably, the volatility of nominal exchange rates is much larger than of real exchange rates (i.e., exchange rates corrected for differences in the price levels in the two economies). As known since Michael Mussa's 1996 paper, *nominal* exchange rate volatility means *real* exchange rate volatility ('Mussa puzzle') – most of the variation in the real exchange rate is in the nominal exchange rate, not in the relative price levels.[19]

Recent research, for example by Xavier Gabaix at New York University and Matteo Maggiori at Harvard University, tries to derive fluctuations in exchange rates from capital flows in highly imperfect, but perhaps more realistic, financial markets, but the implications for the desirability of floating or fixed exchange rates are still to be properly investigated.[20]

The more general point to keep in mind is that exchange rates have a dual nature; they are relative prices between currencies (as emphasised in most theoretical models) but they are also asset prices subject to speculation and arbitrage and traded in liquid markets, and the two roles do not necessarily sit together very well. The euro-dollar exchange rate, for example, can be seen as the price of a basket of goods and services sold in the euro area compared with the same basket sold in the US, and this is what most economic models do. But it is also a speculative asset on which you can gain or lose money – this is how most traders see it, and traders appear to have the upper hand!

Therefore, the question about the excess volatility of exchange rates remains largely unexplained in the economics literature. This may seem like an esoteric matter to the layman, so let me clarify it with an example. Suppose you live in the euro area but are paid in US dollars (say, you work in a US multi-national). The consumer price index that you would care for is the euro area CPI multiplied by the bilateral euro-dollar exchange rate. Because inflation rates are similar in the euro area and the US, there is no reason why a wage paid in US dollars should grow at a substantially different rate than a wage paid in euros. Figure 7.1 reports how much more volatile the bilateral euro/dollar exchange rate is compared with the relative CPI. Whereas the relative CPI moves smoothly in a very narrow band, the euro/dollar exchange rate exhibits wide swings, with deviations from the relative CPI that last several years. It is true that, eventually, the exchange rate reverts back to the Purchasing Power Parity (that is, the level that makes the cost of living the same in the two economies), a fact for which there is significant empirical evidence and which seems to be confirmed by the euro/dollar behaviour over the long term. However, deviations from the PPP last for years, and are large. The impression is that there seems to be an own variability stemming directly, and exogenously, from exchange rate movements, although this needs to be confirmed by rigorous analysis – and in fact there is no consensus yet on this question in the literature.

According to Robert Mundell and others such as Robert Aliber at the University of Chicago, the stabilisation of the euro–dollar exchange rate is the most important priority for the world economy. Free trade requires low volatility

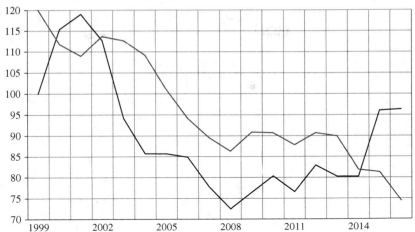

FIGURE 7.1 There is much more variability in the exchange rate than in relative consumer prices in the world's two largest economies, the US and the euro area. Levels are set at 1999 = 100.
Source: Thomson Reuters Datastream, IntLink Database.

in exchange rates; in their view, real exchange rates should not move by more than a few percentage points per year. Intuitively, it seems hard to disagree that the levels of exchange rate volatility that we observe are difficult to explain based on fundamentals.

External adjustment of the balance of payments

Another important dimension to understand the desirability of flexible exchange rates is the adjustment of balance of payments imbalances. Temporary differences between exports and imports are normal and desirable, indeed a sign of optimal consumption smoothing over time (countries that grow faster should borrow more from abroad, expecting to be richer in the future). Countries with faster growth rates, for example, may want to borrow against their future income, which implies a current account deficit. Balance of payments deficits become problematic when the external liability position becomes too large, jeopardising the sustainability of external debt, increasing risk premia and possibly leading to crises and defaults. History is replete with examples of this type of crisis. The question here becomes whether flexible exchange rates are better at making current account imbalances less persistent, and less dangerous for future crises.

How is the external adjustment supposed to work? It depends on the exchange rate regime and the capital controls in place. In fact, the evidence suggests that exchange rates do not eliminate trade imbalances if capital flows are large.[21]

Before looking at external adjustment of trade imbalances in the current international monetary system, it may be useful to pause and look at the experience in previous international monetary systems, starting from the days of the Gold Standard.

External adjustment in the Gold Standard period

In the days of the Gold Standard in the 19th century and early 20th century, the adjustment was relatively easy to understand, and known as the 'specie flow' adjustment. A trade account deficit meant an outflow of gold (capital outflow), which tended to decrease prices in the home country. A lower price level (with exchange rates *de facto* fixed by the Gold Standard) meant cheaper products at home, fostering exports and hindering imports. This in turn restored the balance of payments equilibrium, essentially engineering an internal devaluation (a fall in prices without a depreciation, i.e. entirely through domestic prices). Exchange rates were practically fixed net of gold transport costs, the so-called 'gold points'. There is a good description of this adjustment mechanism already in the works of David Hume in the 18th century.

This adjustment mechanism worked well in the 19th century due to the absence of large imbalances and rather flexible prices. It was much more difficult in the interwar period, with prices and wages less flexible and larger balance of payments imbalances.[22]

External adjustment in the Bretton Woods period

During the Bretton Woods system (dollar standard), countries could be members of the IMF only if their currencies fluctuated in a narrow band around the US dollar. *De facto*, this was a fixed exchange rate international monetary system, though not based on gold (not directly, at least). Short-term imbalances were not a problem because countries could draw on their reserves or access short-term official credit from the IMF. Countries had two ways to face large and prolonged imbalances in the balance of payments, namely, (i) adjusting the peg and (ii) imposing capital controls. Frequently, they did the latter.

External adjustment post-Bretton Woods

After the collapse of the Bretton Woods system in the early 1970s, many countries reverted to flexible exchange rates. In theory, under a flexible exchange rate there is no notion of external imbalance (Mundell-Fleming model). Countries under a peg need to manipulate their foreign exchange reserves to offset movements in private capital flows. For example, a country with a large current account surplus needs to make sure that it increases its foreign exchange reserves and buys foreign currency in order to keep the exchange rate stable. This has led to a large accumulation of foreign exchange reserves especially in emerging countries such as

China, where an undervalued exchange rate has been used as a growth strategy for a decade or more.

But do floating exchange rates really help the adjustment of external imbalances? In a textbook model of international adjustment, flexible exchange rates indeed help the external adjustment. If the Marshall-Lerner conditions are satisfied, the trade balance improves if the exchange rate depreciates. (The Marshall-Lerner conditions state that the trade imbalance improves with depreciation if the quantity effect (stronger demand for exports, weaker demand for imports) prevails over the price effects (imports are more expensive after depreciation).) However, the evidence suggests that floating exchange rates do not help for external adjustment; in particular, the current account adjustment does not appear to be appreciably faster in floating countries, although there is no consensus on this in the literature, and partly depends on the measurement of the exchange rate regime, which is subject to error.[23]

In a fixed exchange rate arrangement the country can adjust relative prices and achieve international competitiveness – in turn improving its net export performance – only by reducing domestic prices (or letting them increase less than those of its competitors). This process of internal devaluation may be very costly if prices are sticky or, in the case of wages, rigid downwards. There are not many estimates, however, of just how much more costly internal devaluations are compared with external devaluations centred on the nominal exchange rate. However, the experience of the adjustment in some euro area countries, notably Greece, would suggest that internal devaluation may entail significant macroeconomic costs and hardship.

Emerging markets pay attention to the exchange rate, in particular to appreciation, even when they do not say so explicitly. One key reason is that they are perceived to be periodically hit by shocks to capital flows, often influenced by market sentiment or factors related to creditor countries (such as their monetary policy) rather than by their own fundamentals or policies, which they can control at least to some extent. These waves of capital flows have the potential to both appreciate and depreciate the exchange rate in a way that can be disruptive.

One particularly difficult situation is when 'excessive' inflows determine an undue appreciation of the currency in an emerging market, which shifts resources towards non-tradables, namely goods that cannot be traded internationally. This can unduly damage the tradable sector, such as manufacturing, which is often the motor of growth and innovation and the sector that is less sheltered from competition or less close to the political sphere. This is often referred to as the 'Dutch disease', which takes its name from the boom in natural gas in the Netherlands in the 1990s, which displaced the manufacturing sector. It is more typical of emerging markets that discover natural resources, or produce natural resources that are suddenly more in demand. The higher demand for natural resources diverts capital away from other sectors, in particular manufacturing, and makes the country less competitive due to appreciation.

More generally, the international community (not only emerging markets but also economists in advanced countries and international institutions such as the IMF) are reviewing their previously optimistic assessment of unfettered capital flows, in particular short-term and volatile portfolio flows, and also more generally of financial integration and globalisation, namely that capital is globally mobile and markets are more correlated internationally. There is much more tolerance than there used to be for measures aimed at preventing excessive volatility in capital flows, such as capital controls, and this is also a new element of the international monetary system.

The valuation channel

Exchange rates are relevant not only for trade in goods and services, but also for trade in financial assets. With the rapid growth in foreign assets and liabilities, the importance of the so-called 'valuation channel' is also increasing over time. Essentially, exchange rate movements create financial gains and losses. If a country has, say, more foreign currency assets than liabilities, currency depreciation is normally a capital gain, which can be expansionary through wealth effects (citizens feel richer and therefore spend more, fostering economic activity). The sign and magnitude of this effect depends on the composition of countries' international balance sheets, on which the data are patchy. For some countries, in particular emerging countries, the sign is negative: hence depreciation leads to valuation losses.

If a country is running a sizeable trade imbalance, exchange rate movements may contribute to its adjustment in two ways. First, there is a trade channel: depreciation increases net exports. Second, there are valuation effects: depreciation changes the country's net wealth vs. the rest of the world. If a country is net short in foreign currency (say, its debt is dollarised), it may well lose from a depreciation of the domestic currency – its debt burden may go up, or its foreign assets decline in value.

This question is closely connected to the literature on the so-called 'original sin': this is not the Biblical version, but says that developing countries with poor institutions and low monetary policy credibility (e.g., who cannot enforce central bank independence) are forced to issue debt in foreign currency, in particular when selling assets to foreign investors (foreign banks), resulting in currency mismatches. These countries may end up being short in foreign currency (more liabilities than assets in foreign currency), and a depreciation may entail negative wealth effects (in particular, an increase in the real debt burden). This mechanism was very much at play during the Asian crisis in the late 1990s.

The normative question: the OCA theory

At this point it is useful to revisit the question posed at the beginning: when should a group of countries abandon floating exchange rates and move to a fixed exchange rate system among them? What are the main costs and benefits? The traditional theory (Robert Mundell's Optimum Currency Area theory, known as OCA) says that a region where it is optimal to have a single currency should be one where:

- factors of production (e.g. labour) are mobile; for example, it is easy for workers to move across borders;
- shocks are correlated; for example, recessions and booms are correlated across countries;
- the economic structures are similar; say, all countries are strong in manufacturing while they are commodity importers.

This is a useful framework for organising thoughts but it is not really an operational one. It is not easy to say whether each of these preconditions is satisfied, if not in qualitative terms. It also does not take into account what we now know about exchange rates and their role in financial adjustment, in particular. Moreover, it could be argued that some of the criteria (e.g. similar economic structures) are endogenous, so that a group of countries joining a fixed exchange rate arrangement or a monetary union can become an OCA *ex post* if they are not an OCA *ex ante* ('endogenous OCA').[24] Certainly the OCA theory was mentioned often during the period before the introduction of the euro, but historically it did not play an important role in the creation of the common currency, which overwhelmingly reflected political factors.[25] Moreover, this is a good theory given the knowledge of the 1960s; we now know much more on the role of exchange rates as channels of adjustment, so the OCA theory is in need of a thorough update.

Does it matter what exchange rate regime is chosen?

Do we know what determines countries' exchange rate regime choice, independent of whether the choice is optimal? Certainly size plays a role – most countries in the world are small and they prefer a fixed exchange rate regime, for obvious reasons. It is difficult to run an independent monetary policy, and small countries may not have enough qualified personnel or resources to run it properly. Moreover, all large rich countries float. Apart from this, we do not really know much about the drivers of the choice of the exchange rate regime. For example, it is not clear why, say, Denmark chooses to peg, and Sweden to float. Even the evidence on the role of the quality of the institutions is mixed.

We do not know much about the drivers of the choice of the exchange rate regime, but does it have material consequences for countries? In fact, there is not much systematic evidence that the choice of the exchange rate regime matters for the variables policy-makers should care for, such as economic growth and inflation. There is some evidence that hard pegs lead to lower inflation, but only in emerging countries, based on the argument that in this way they 'buy credibility' from the institutions of richer countries. Almost all rich countries float and practically all of them enjoy low inflation and high central bank credibility. Denmark pegs its exchange rate and Sweden does not, Hong Kong pegs but Singapore does not, but they do not seem to have major differences in their economic structures and performance.[26]

Another important element to understand the costs and benefits of pegging exchange rates is whether the exchange rate regime makes countries more or less exposed to speculative attacks in the form of volatility portfolio flows. It was argued that countries in an intermediate regime (managed floating) were actually more exposed to this risk, leading to a 'bipolarity claim': better either to peg or to float fully. This is confirmed in recent work, which however finds that hard pegs do not protect from certain types of crises, in particular growth collapses. Floats appear to have the best performance in terms of reduced vulnerability to crises.[27]

There is more to central banking than interest rates and exchange rates

So far we have discussed the question of the desirability of a world central bank mainly from the point of view of monetary policy. Nobody can deny, of course, that monetary policy is the first order question, but there is much more to central banking than monetary policy proper. This should be considered as well when thinking about the potential benefits of a world currency.

As seen, central banks have a crucial role as lender of last resort in the domestic economy. But if foreign debt is in foreign currency, the domestic central bank is not in a good position to be a lender of last resort. It could certainly create domestic currency and buy foreign currency in the forex market, but this would probably depreciate the domestic currency and possibly exacerbate the problem, notably through valuation effects. At the international level, we need a supranational lender of last resort.

The IMF is not a central bank and cannot create money in an unlimited way. Hence, it cannot be said that the IMF is akin to a global central bank. It cannot undertake open market operations and influence global liquidity conditions. Moreover, the IMF can only lend to governments, not to banks (central banks, on the other hand, sometimes cannot lend to governments). Were the world to move to a world currency, a profound change in the international monetary system would be required, including allowing the IMF (or a global central bank) to provide emergency lending to financial intermediaries and possibly governments all over the world. More generally, there is much more to global central banking than fixing exchange rates, as the recent experience of the euro area has surely demonstrated.

A final point worth noting is that a fixed currency arrangement and even more so a monetary union implies the loss, for each individual country, of the ability to inflate away public debt. Presumably, a world central bank will not care much about fiscal sustainability in one of the over 200 members, and will not bend its policies for that eventuality. For individual countries in a world monetary union, the fiscal theory of the price level just cannot be correct! A consequence of this is that, in these countries, high public debt can be corrected only by running primary surpluses or by defaulting. Monetary dominance becomes unavoidable, and this is not necessarily the best option available in all circumstances, as we saw in Chapter 3.

To sum up, exchange rates are certainly excessively volatile and they do not appear to play the smooth adjustment role that Friedman envisaged some 60 years ago. The evidence on their usefulness is mixed at best. At the same time, to build a world monetary union or at least an international monetary system based on fixed exchange rates is a daunting task, with uncertain benefits and a long list of open questions. At a minimum, the world will need evidence that a monetary union works in a sustainable way in the euro area before even thinking about embarking on such a project at the world level. Moreover, before thinking of going the full way towards a world currency a reform of the international monetary system with some more diversification away from, and less dependence on, the US dollar may be on the cards.

Notes

1 There is a large literature on the determinants of international currencies (which factors determine whether a country has an international currency); a seminar contribution is Krugman, P., 'The International Role of the Dollar: Theory and Prospect', in Bilson, J. and R. Marston (eds.), *Exchange Rate Theory and Practice*, Chicago: University of Chicago Press, 1984, pp. 261–278. Economies of scale are important in the international context as they are domestically; it is more efficient to have one or at most very few monetary standards.
2 For an excellent review of the history of the international monetary system see McKinnon, R., 'The rules of the game: International money in historical perspective', *Journal of Economic Literature*, XXXI, 1993, 1–44.
3 An excellent account of the Bretton Woods conference is Steil, B., *The Battle of Bretton Woods*, Princeton: Princeton University Press, 2010.
4 It was not a proposal for a world currency with a global central bank, it was rather the creation of a supranational currency and only as a unit of account, not means of payment. The Bancor would be issued by an International Clearing Union, convertible into all national currencies at a fixed exchange rate. Importantly, countries could have borrowed from the Clearing Union in Bancor, up to a certain limit. In order to facilitate external adjustment, countries would have been charged an interest (in a symmetric way, i.e. including surplus countries) if they deviated too much from a zero balance.
5 Differently from the current situation with the Trump presidency, at the time it was Britain, not the US, that was worried about persistent trade deficits.
6 Bordo and McCauley (2017), however, warn not to over-do the use of the Triffin dilemma and to adapt it to any circumstance and problem; see Bordo, M. D. and R. N. McCauley, 'Triffin: Dilemma or Myth?', Bank for International Settlements Working Paper 684, 2017.
7 Bloomfield, A. I., 'Monetary Policy under the International Gold Standard, 1880–1914', Federal Reserve Bank of New York, 1959.
8 For example, Hong Kong has a currency board arrangement with the US dollar, and Bulgaria with the euro.
9 Di Giovanni, J. and J. Shambaugh, 'The Impact of Foreign Interest Rates on the Economy: The Role of the Exchange Rate Regime', *Journal of International Economics* 74, 2, 2008, 341–361.

10. Dedola, L., Rivolta, G. and L. Stracca, 'If the Fed Sneezes, Who Catches a Cold?', *Journal of International Economics*, 108(S1), 2017, 23–41.
11. Feenstra, R., Luck, P., Obstfeld, M. and K. Russ, 'In Search of the Armington Elasticity', NBER Working Paper 20063, 2014.
12. Friedman, M., 'The Case for Flexible Exchange Rates', in M. Friedman (eds.), *Essays in Positive Economics*, Chicago: University of Chicago Press, 1953, 157–203.
13. See Broda, C., 'Terms of Trade and Exchange Rate Regimes in Developing Countries', *Journal of International Economics* 63, 1, 2004, 31–58.
14. Ramcharan, R., 'Cataclysms and Currencies; Does the Exchange Rate Regime Matter for Real Shocks?', IMF Working Paper 05/85, 2005.
15. Burstein, A. and G. Gopinath, 'International Prices and Exchange Rates', Chapter 7, *Handbook of International Economics*, Elsevier, 2014, 391–451.
16. Corsetti, G. and P. Pesenti, 'The Simple Geometry of Transmission and Stabilization in Closed and Open Economies', NBER Working Paper 11341, 2005.
17. See Devereux, M. and C. Engel, 'Monetary Policy in the Open Economy Revisited: Price Setting and Exchange Rate Flexibility', *Review of Economic Studies* 70, 2003, 765–84.
18. Corsetti and Pesenti (op. cit.).
19. Mussa, M., 'Nominal Exchange Rate Regimes and the Behaviour of Real Exchange Rates: Evidence and Implications', *Carnegie-Rochester Series on Public Policy* 25, 1996, 117–214.
20. Gabaix, X. and M. Maggiori, 'International Liquidity and Exchange Rate Dynamics', *The Quarterly Journal of Economics* 130, 3, 2015, 1369–1420.
21. See, e.g., Sardoni, C. and L. R. Wray, 'Fixed and Flexible Exchange Rates and Currency Sovereignty', The Levy Institute of Bard College Working Paper 489, 2007.
22. O'Rourke, K. and A. Taylor, 'Cross of Euros', *Journal of Economic Perspectives* 27, 3, 2013, 167–92.
23. See Chinn, M. and S.-J. Wei, 'A Faith-Based Initiative Meets the Evidence: Does a Flexible Exchange Rate Regime Really Facilitate Current Account Adjustment?', *The Review of Economics and Statistics* 95, 1, 2013, 168–184.
24. Frankel, J. and A. Rose, 'The Endogeneity of the Optimum Currency Area Criteria', *Economic Journal* 108, 1998, 1009–1025.
25. This in turn implies that the OCA theory is not a good theory of how monetary unions, such as the monetary union in the euro area, come into existence. See C. A. E. Goodhart, 'The two concepts of money: implications for the analysis of optimal currency areas', European Journal of Political Economy, 14, 3, 407–432, 1998.
26. Rose, A. K., 'Exchange Rate Regimes in the Modern Era: Fixed, Floating, and Flaky', *Journal of Economic Literature* 49, 3, 2011, 652–672.
27. Ghosh, A., Ostry, J. and M. S. Qureshi, 'Exchange Rate Management and Crisis Susceptibility: A Reassessment', *IMF Economic Review* 63, 1, 2015, 238–276.

8

WILL CENTRAL BANKS DISAPPEAR?

Central banks, like other public institutions, are in a state of constant evolution and their role does not remain fixed over time. There is the temptation to argue that today's consensus (central bank as an independent institution with narrow focus on price stability using an interest rate instrument, lender of last resort under the Bagehot doctrine) will last forever, but most likely it will not.

We have seen that central banks have been born in most cases as private institutions, which were not at all neutral, for example in their credit allocation, and mostly pursued a private interest. They have often favoured particular sectors and focused on economic development rather than price stability – some central banks in emerging countries indeed still do that.[1]

Different views on the benefit of central banks

The evolution of central banks in the last two centuries can be seen in different ways, but there is at least a current of thought that this is an overall benign evolution (we will come back to this view at the end of this chapter). Lawrence Broz, at the University of California at San Diego, is of the view that the evolution of central banks combined, in a socially beneficial way, rent seeking from the central bankers (a private interest) with a public interest. This is epitomised, in particular, by the evolution of the first major central bank, the Bank of England, which rose from a rent-seeking private institution to become, in the middle of the 19th century, an institution with mainly a public interest and which was the guardian of the then-dominant British financial system.[2] This view sees the evolution of central banks as a quid pro quo between cheap financing for governments and rents for the (central) bankers, which is sometimes referred to as the 'fiscal theory' of the origin of central banks.

But there is also another current of thought that sees central banks as another example of central planning and an expropriation by the government, which derives rents from issuing fiat money. This current of criticism of central banks is particularly strong in the United States, which has had a more troubled central banking history than other advanced countries and has a strong federal tradition.[3] Central banks in Europe are also sometimes subject to intense criticism for their policies, but there is less criticism towards the existence of the institution as such. With the global financial crisis, criticism of central banks has spread to the blogosphere – some bloggers, for example, claim that central banks are there to serve the '1 per cent', or that they are part of a world conspiracy, and so forth.

Interestingly, the idea of a central bank associated with a conspiracy of the elites ('monied interests') against the common citizen has an old history in the US. Andrew Jackson, US president between 1829 and 1837, successfully campaigned for the abolition of the Second Bank of the United States, and the Bank became a central issue in the presidential campaign of 1832, a struggle known as the 'bank war'. The press at the time showed images of Andrew Jackson slaying the hydra of the Second Bank of the United States – maybe some US politicians still now see the Federal Reserve in a similar way. Eventually, Jackson was successful in his endeavour and the establishment of a central bank in the United States had to wait for another 80 years, until the bank panic of 1907 finally convinced everybody that the establishment of a central bank was overdue.[4]

One could dismiss this criticism as largely irrelevant for the actual conduct of monetary policy, but some of it is healthy and sometimes has good arguments. For example, the claim that the Federal Reserve and other central banks are too dominant in the academic field of central banking and monetary economics, thus (unwillingly) quashing or preventing dissent, may have an element of truth.[5] Moreover, society has a right to choose its monetary institutions in full freedom and after listening to all the arguments. What is important is that criticism does not become an a priori one, devoid of good arguments and content, and it is not too subject to the vagaries of the political debate. In his 2009 book *End the Fed*, US congressman Ron Paul makes some good observations, but then goes off track to argue that current US monetary policy will lead to hyper-inflation. US presidential candidate Ted Cruz has advocated ending the Fed and going back to the Gold Standard. There is a fine line, difficult to identify with precision, between central bank accountability to the political sphere (generally to parliaments), which is to be welcomed, and jeopardising central bank independence, which is not. For example, the 'Audit the Fed' bill, which would allow the US Government Accountability Office to 'monitor' US monetary policy, has raised some concerns from this point of view.

On the side of more credible criticism, outlets such as the *Cato Journal* contain good arguments and rigorous criticisms both of the Federal Reserve actions and of the existence of the Federal Reserve as a public institution or central planner. As far as I know, no such outlet exists in Europe or Japan, where the central bank is generally taken for granted as an institution.

As already mentioned in Chapter 1, a quite worrying trend in the wake of the global financial crisis is the decline in trust in central banks, as measured in surveys such as the Eurobarometer survey in Europe.[6] It is not clear if this reflects a more generalised decline in policy-making institutions or public authorities, or the decline is more pronounced for central banks. The decline in trust is notable also because central banks used to enjoy relatively high levels of public trust, normally higher than other public institutions. This decline in trust needs to be better addressed and understood – over time, an independent and unelected institution cannot perform optimally without a high degree of trust. Communication is probably key in fostering trust and major central banks are in fact investing heavily in this domain.

The knowledge problem

One core criticism of central banks builds on the idea that they are central planners and, like all central planners, they are subject to the 'knowledge problem' – they do not have enough information to decide on the optimal allocation of scarce resources and they do not know the underlying determinants of the macroeconomic variables they care for, even if they are well intentioned (not to be taken for granted). This view has quite a long tradition in the history of economic thought, but it is best expressed in the writing of Friedrich Hayek, a free market advocate who won the Nobel Prize in economics in 1974. In his truly excellent Nobel lecture, 'The Pretence of Knowledge'[7], Hayek argues for example that:

> Unlike the position that exists in the physical sciences, in economics and other disciplines that deal with essentially complex phenomena, the aspects of the events to be accounted for about which we can get quantitative data are necessarily limited and may not include the important ones. While in the physical sciences it is generally assumed, probably with good reason, that any important factor which determines the observed events will itself be directly observable and measurable, in the study of such complex phenomena as the market, which depend on the actions of many individuals, all the circumstances which will determine the outcome of a process, for reasons which I shall explain later, will hardly ever be fully known or measurable. And while in the physical sciences the investigator will be able to measure what, on the basis of a prima facie theory, he thinks important, in the social sciences often that is treated as important which happens to be accessible to measurement. This is sometimes carried to the point where it is demanded that our theories must be formulated in such terms that they refer only to measurable magnitudes.

In short, economists and social scientists don't really know what they are talking about. As so do central bankers. And who can deny that there is a large amount of uncertainty regarding the economy, especially those who work or have worked in policy making institutions?

The next question is what to do with the knowledge problem. One possibility is to make decisions with the best of the knowledge we have, knowing those decisions will be less than perfect but still hopefully the best possible ones. I would characterise this as the mainstream view.

But there are two other ways to deal with the knowledge problem. One first line of thought suggests that, faced with the knowledge problem, central banks should follow rules, such as the Taylor rule. This is the view that can be first associated with Milton Friedman (although Friedman never expressed it, at least explicitly, as a solution to the knowledge problem) and lives on with the views of, for example, John Taylor at Stanford University. Monetary policy should broadly follow a well-defined policy rule – not to avoid the 'time inconsistency' as we saw in Chapter 2, but because tinkering with the economy in a discretionary manner will lead to disaster due to lack of knowledge (or pretence of knowledge) by the central bankers.[8]

A more radical view, expressed brilliantly in Friedrich Hayek's book *The Denationalisation of Money*, is that monetary policy should be set in a competitive manner, and not by a central planner like the central bank.[9] The central planner has no idea of the right level of a market price, which the nominal interest rate is, so let the market – which is good at that – identify that level and aggregate the dispersed and tacit information of market participants.

Is currency competition a force for good?

Hayek argues that we should remove the government monopoly in the issuance of outside money, and competition between different possible outside monies should be possible. His central argument is that competition will provide the more stable currency – just as it provides the best cars or the best computers. Monetary entrepreneurship can be good.

One important argument made by Hayek is that Gresham's law will not apply in a situation of currency competition. Let us recall that Gresham's law says that bad money will chase away good money, so only bad money will circulate in equilibrium, whereas good money will be hoarded. Not so, says Hayek – Gresham's law only applies if there is a fixed, government-set relative price between two currencies, say gold and silver. If this restriction is removed, competition will make sure that the relative price between two monies moves in order to equalise the opportunity of holding each of them. As a result, it will not necessarily be more convenient to hold gold and give away silver, so that both will circulate and not only one of them.

The problem with currency competition

Hayek's proposal is bold and has a certain appeal. We know that the market is a superior allocation mechanism compared with the government. Haven't capitalist societies fared better than communist countries after all?

Not so fast. Competition is certainly good in general, and economists always emphasise its benefits, but it is not obviously so for something that is likely to be a natural monopoly and where network externalities are strong. 'Network externalities' sounds like a complicated concept but it is actually pretty simple: it says that it is more advantageous to use a certain product or standard if others also use it. For example, in a country where English is the main language it is advantageous for a new resident to learn that language as opposed to, say, Vietnamese. The QWERTY keyboard is another common example. Network externalities have a number of implications, most notably the staying power of existing standards – it is not easy to replace the incumbent even if it is clearly sub-optimal (which is probably the case for the QWERTY keyboard from which I am writing this).

Where Hayek has, in my view, the right concern is that private sector participants may bring up new ideas on how an ideal monetary system could be, and in this they could possibly be better than academics and almost certainly better than government officials. In the hands of the government, there is a risk that money supply is not innovative, and there may be better monies out there that society will never experience. However, there are three important problems with currency competition.

First, as already noted long ago by Milton Friedman and Anna Schwartz, there is really no legal monopoly for government issued outside money in most countries.[10] Sometimes the law specifies that a certain currency is legal tender and has to be accepted as payment, but also never says that payment in other forms is not accepted. If there was a better form of money out there, it would have probably already arisen, but it has not.[11] A counter-argument to this criticism is that governments want taxes to be paid in government issued money, which tilts the odds in its favour because taxes are a large part of household payments.

Second, money is a solution to a collective action problem – it is a public good. We know that the market is not very good at solving that problem – it is difficult for the market to coordinate society on a solution. Imagine if the choice was what language to speak in a country. How could a decentralised system come up with a solution, and can we be sure that the solution would be the right one? For example, English is the global language, arisen from a largely decentralised process. Can we say that it is an optimal global language – especially in its pidgin version 'global English'? And indeed, we can make the same argument with the international monetary system, which is a place where currency competition already exists. We have seen that the 'market' solution has simply been to adopt the currency of the biggest country, the US dollar, without providing too much entrepreneurship and innovation. We cannot trust that a more virtuous process would prevail at the domestic level, if currency competition was fostered.

Indeed, what we observe at domestic level is high persistence of a monetary standard which lasts until that form of money (typically government issued fiat money) is severely mismanaged, for example with very high inflation. Only in that case the existing monetary standard can be supplanted by other standards, including privately supplied commodities.[12] But you need a really spectacular failure to see that type of substitution – otherwise, domestic currency has a remarkable staying power.[13]

Third, experiences with the closest historical experiences to currency competition, for example 'free banking' in the US in the 19th century, or periods of monetary instability when different forms of money circulated, were more periods of chaos rather than of monetary innovation. Indeed, free banking was so unworkable that it led to the creation of the Federal Reserve System.

There are also other problems with currency competition, for example, parasitic currencies (how to avoid that the best currency has imitators, which dilute its supply and undermine its qualities). The main point I want to convey here is that the proposal of currency competition has less appeal than it seems at first sight, but it would be wrong to entirely forget about Hayek's insight. There is a distinct risk that there is less innovation in monetary matters than would be desirable, and we should not trust the government to necessarily know better.

Is there empirical evidence to bear on this question?

Do we know if central banks do any good? A relevant empirical test would be to compare countries with or without central banks for exogenous reasons. If we could run experiments in economics, we would choose 100 countries and randomly assign a central bank to 50 of them, while keeping the others without, and then see the results. Unfortunately, most countries do have central banks now and they don't seem to be ready to be involved in such an experiment. There is some limited empirical analysis, but it mostly concerns the 19th century and is heavily influenced by the British experience with a central bank, which was largely positive. A recent issue of the *Cato Journal*, entitled 'Was the Fed a good idea?', however, reflects a variety of views with an overall mixed message.

Digital currencies: Hayek's vindication?

In recent years there has been a lot of talk about digital currencies, in particular Bitcoin. Are they a new competitor of central banks, and can they vindicate Hayek?

Digital currencies are precisely what Hayek had in mind. They are an alternative monetary system in competition with government produced fiat money, with a floating exchange rate vs. the main currencies. They may be seen as the most credible alternative to central bank money.[14] Are they ripe for that?

Bitcoin (and other digital currencies like it) have been designed by engineers, not economists. Therefore, they are not necessarily, by design, an optimal monetary system which the readers of this book would recognise. At the same time, the way Bitcoin is designed is reminiscent of a commodity standard, and has some of the advantages that economists typically associate with it. The key difference, of course, is that Bitcoin exists only in the virtual world and is not associated with a physical commodity – it is rather an intangible commodity.

There is a limited supply of Bitcoin, with a long-term ceiling (21 million Bitcoins), and it is costly to 'mine' Bitcoin. Mining is done electronically, by solving puzzles that are costly to unlock but easy to verify. Bitcoin is built on the block-chain technology, which is a way to collectively verify transactions. The block-chain technology is essentially a distributed ledger, whereby private transactions are publicly validated.[15] 'Seignorage' accrues to whoever verifies the transaction, which requires significant computing power.

The beauty of the block-chain technology is that it potentially solves a problem that has vexed all credit based systems as an alternative to barter. In fact, we have seen already in the first chapter that it is not easy to ensure that a register of all transactions is properly maintained. If I sell you a good, you (as the debtor in the transaction) have every interest that the transaction is entirely forgotten one second after it is carried out. Any form of credit-based money therefore requires that the system used to record transactions is credible for all. But who controls the controller? Any centralised system may be subject to manipulation or loss. The block-chain technology allows third parties to verify the transaction once and for all, gaining some Bitcoin in doing that. Once the transaction is verified, it is stored so that it cannot be changed thereafter without changing all transactions coming after it (hence the 'chain' term in the name). It is a peer-to-peer network that aims at reaching consensus on the history of transactions. The technology allowing this is built on new developments in public-private key cryptography.

Is Bitcoin, in its present form, a credible contender to central bank money? Probably not, for at least three reasons.

First and foremost, there is not monetary policy to speak of. If anything, Bitcoin resembles the Gold Standard – a system that we have collectively abandoned for a good reason.

Second, it is a system that consumes a lot of electrical power. Mining Bitcoin is not only privately costly, but also publicly costly for the environment. It seems a quite wasteful way to establish an alternative monetary standard. Moreover, transactions tend to take time, which is not ideal if the purpose of any monetary standard is to minimise transaction costs. Actually, it has been shown that congestion and delays are crucial for raising revenue for miners and attracting them, and hence for the system to remain viable![16]

Third, even if Bitcoin was an excellent monetary standard, it would take a lot of time for people to switch if they are used to an old standard. People who are used to paper currency, in particular, may find the online use of Bitcoin off-putting or even frightening. This is an example of the more general point that for goods where network externalities are strong one cannot expect the best product to prevail, at least in the short term. Path dependency is key.

Perhaps reflecting these limitations, Bitcoin remains a very small market (around 14 billion USD as outstanding amount) and is more seen as a speculative investment rather than a payment system, apart from some niches. The price of Bitcoin vs. established currencies such as the EUR or the USD fluctuates wildly, more than is usual for exchange rates.

Self-correcting monetary standards

Another alternative to central banking is a mechanism that automatically ensures price stability – because the monetary standard is itself defined in terms of a basket of goods and services. This scheme, sometimes called 'Greenfield-Yaeger scheme', is a system where a bundle of commodities is the unit of account, and it may be detached from the means of payment – which can be paper currencies.[17] If the bundle is large enough, the monetary standard may automatically ensure price stability in a way that a commodity standard – where the relative price fluctuates for factors related to a particular market – cannot achieve. The unit of account can be defined by the government.

With such a self-correcting monetary standard monetary policy would be run by an autopilot. A recent study shows how the central bank can implement such a scheme even within the current monetary system, by paying an inflation-indexed rate of return on central bank reserves that define the unit of account.[18]

I believe this scheme is interesting and should be studied more. One key advantage of this scheme is that it would automatically make nominal contracts real. This would eliminate some of the frictions that monetary policy seeks to (very imperfectly) address, such as sticky prices and debt deflation. They would also be a solution that is robust to mismanagement of monetary policy, which can happen indeed even to the best intentioned central bank, taking into account the complexity of the economy and model uncertainty. But it seems to me that this scheme suffers from the same limitation as the Eisler proposal to eliminate the ZLB problem, namely the need to separate the unit of account and the means of payment functions of money. Until we are able to design a means of payment that fluctuates in value and can be tied to a Greenfield-Yaeger scheme – which probably requires the elimination of paper currency – this will always be a considerable downside of this kind of proposal.

A final look at the data

It seems appropriate to end this book by taking a long view at the historical experience. Figure 8.1 reports CPI inflation in the United States – the country with perhaps the best historical data in the world and also with one of the most diverse experiences in different monetary standards. The horizontal line marks 2% inflation, which is now considered as the inflation target in the United States and around most of the world.

The US monetary system evolved from a bimetallic standard for most of the 19th century to a gold standard, officially established in 1900 with the Gold Standard Act. The Federal Reserve was established in 1913. During World War I, convertibility of the dollar into gold was suspended twice, in order to allow for higher government debt due to the war expenditure. After returning to the Gold Standard, the US experienced the Great Depression, which eventually led to abandoning the

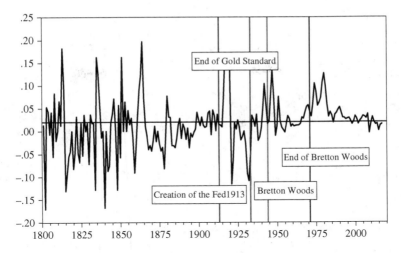

FIGURE 8.1 CPI inflation in the United States, 1800 to present.
Source: Global financial data.

Gold Standard in 1933, with the Gold Reserve Act. After a period when the dollar was left freely floating, with the Bretton Woods conference in 1944 the Gold Exchange Standard re-established a link between the dollar and gold, which lasted until 1971. The period since the early 1970s is the fiat money regime, when the liabilities of the Federal Reserve represent the only form of outside money – as is the case in practically all other countries.

What does the inflation record say? I would draw four conclusions when looking at the inflation data since 1800. First, inflation was much more volatile especially in the first part of the 1800s, probably reflecting the fact that agricultural prices dominated in that period, and these were very volatile mainly due to weather conditions. Second, deflation has been a common occurrence, and the US was in deflation (again as several other industrial countries) for most of the second half of the 19th century. Third, inflation and deflation punctuated key salient episodes such as the two World Wars and the Great Depression. Fourth, and most important for the present chapter, inflation has been most stable during the fiat money period, especially after the early 1980s (the Volcker dis-inflation). Admittedly the Federal Reserve (and other central banks) needed a period of 'learning' during which inflation largely escaped its control in the 1970s, the period of the Great Inflation. But since the Fed has 'learnt' its lesson – and again it is important to emphasise that this is a phenomenon that extends to other rich countries – inflation has been low and stable. It is striking to note the difference between the deflation during the Great Depression and the muted fall in inflation during the global financial crisis of 2007–09, a shock of similar magnitude. Any monetary system alternative to central banks has to beat this performance – not that it is impossible, but it is pretty good by historical standards, at least according to this metric.

A final word

We are not at the end of history of central banks – their current configuration is not an end point and is bound to evolve. With that observation in mind, I would submit that three issues are key looking forward – especially if central banks want to remain in business for the long haul.

First, central banks need to solve the zero bound problem, hopefully without waiting for paper currency to disappear. And it should be a full solution, not a partial solution such as non-standard policies.

Second, the profession at large needs to develop a better understanding of boom and bust cycles in credit and asset prices, as well as the role of central banks in them. Mitigating booms and busts and preventing financial crises should top of the list of any policy-maker, but it is existential for central banks.

Finally, central banks need to be innovative and be open to different monetary standards – in fact I have identified self-correcting fiat money as probably the most innovative one. The fact that they interact so productively and continuously with academics is a good sign, but there is always the risk of inertia and groupthink. If they can remain agile and innovative, they can continue to play a key role in the provision of money, which is such an essential infrastructure of a modern economy. Addressing hard questions such as dealing with the zero bound and preventing booms and busts in asset prices require fresh and clear thinking, certainly not an inertial or defensive attitude.

Notes

1 Epstein, G., *Central Banks as Agents of Economic Development*, Helsinki: UNU World Institute for Development Economics, 2005.
2 Broz, J. L., 'The Origins of Central Banks: Solutions to the Free Rider Problem', *International Organization* 52, 2, 1998.
3 There were two unsuccessful attempts to create a central bank in the United States in the 19th century, the First and the Second Bank of the United States. Both lasted only relatively shortly, and their mandates were not renewed. For a history of the creation of the Federal Reserve see Lowenstein, R., *America's Bank: The Epic Struggle to Create the Federal Reserve*, New York: Penguin Press.
4 Other factors may have been at play in the establishment of the Federal Reserve. Broz (2009) also argues that international factors were also important in the establishment of the Federal Reserve, in particular to foster the international use of the dollar in competition with the British pound and London; see Broz, J. L., *The International Origins of the Federal Reserve System*, Ithaca: Cornell University Press, 2009. Beyond the lack of an international role for the dollar, another problem that was very visible before the creation of the Federal Reserve was the wild fluctuations in interest rates, partly due to seasonal factors. The creation of the Federal Reserve partly eliminated the seasonal fluctuations in interest rates, which were strong beforehand; see Carlson, M. and D. C. Wheelock, 'Did the Founding of the Federal Reserve Affect the Vulnerability of the Interbank System to Systemic Risk?', Finance and Economics Discussion Series, Federal Reserve Board, 2016–059, 2016.
5 See Grim, R., 'Priceless: How the Federal Reserve Bought the Economics Profession', 23 October 2009, http://www.huffingtonpost.com/2009/09/07/priceless-how-the-federal_n_278805.html.

6. Farvaque, E., Hayat, M. A. and A. Mihailov, 'Who Supports the ECB? Evidence from the Eurobarometer Survey', *The World Economy* 40, 4, 2016, 654–677.
7. Later published as von Hayek, F., 'The Pretence of Knowledge', *American Economic Review*, 79, 6, 1989, 3–7.
8. See G. P. O'Driscoll, 'Monetary Policy and the Knowledge Problem', *Cato Journal* 36, 2, 2016.
9. Von Hayek, F., *The Denationalisation of Money*, London: Institute of Economic Affairs, 1976.
10. Friedman, M. and A. Schwartz, 'Has government any Role in Money?', in A. Schwartz (eds.), *Money in Historical Perspective*, Chicago: University of Chicago Press, 1987.
11. It is impossible to resist reporting the usual economist joke: An economist and a normal person are walking down the street together. The normal person says 'Hey, look, there's a $20 bill on the sidewalk!' The economist replies by saying, 'That's impossible – if it were really a $20 bill, it would have been picked up by now'.
12. In Russia after the collapse of the Soviet Union, for example, even barter was widely used. One famous case is the exchange between PepsiCo and the 'Stoli' Russian Vodka.
13. Leijonhufvud, A., 'High Inflations and Contemporary Monetary Theory', University of California, Los Angeles Working Paper 638, 1991.
14. For a good review of Bitcoin see Böhme, R., Christin, N., Edelman, B. and T. Moore, 'Bitcoin: Economics, Technology, and Governance', *Journal of Economics Perspectives* 29, 2, 2015, 213–38.
15. See Dwyer, G. P., 'Blockchain: A Primer', MPRA Paper 76562, 2016.
16. Huberman, G., J. D. Lesotho and C. C. Moallemi, 'Monopoly without a Monopolist: An Economic Analysis of the Bitcoin Payment System', CEPR Discussion Paper 12322, 2017.
17. Greenfield, R. L. and L. B. Yaeger, 'A Laissez-faire Approach to Monetary Stability', *Journal of Money, Credit and Banking* 15, 3, 1983, 302–315.
18. Hall, R. E. and R. Reis, 'Achieving Price Stability by Manipulating the Central Bank's Payment on Reserves', NBER Working Paper No. 22761, 2016.

INDEX

A reference in *italics* indicates a figure and tables are shown in **bold**.

asymmetric information 4, 74, 75, 84

Bagehot, Walter 83
balance sheets: under the Gold Standard 11; government bonds on during QE 62; losses on 62–3; size of in the main industrialised countries *62*; stylised balance sheets **11**
Banca d'Italia 39
Bancor 104
bank default risks 73
bank deposits: the Great Depression as run on 81; as key function of banks 76–7; liquidity transformation 77, 80
Bank of England: establishment of 10; evolution of 119; use of LOLR function 84
bank runs: deposit insurance against 81; equilibria for 79–80; fire sale externalities 79, 83; implications of 79; lender of last resort (LOLR) function and 81; overview of 78–9; sunspot equilibria 79
banks: evolution of 76; fragility of 79–80; leverage 77–8; limited liability 78; liquidity transformation 77, 80
Barro-Gordon model of central bank independence 36
barter systems 3, 4, 5
Benhabib, Jess 51
Bernanke, Ben 60, 80, 86, 89

Bitcoin: as alternative to central bank money 125; block-chain technology 125; overview of 93, 124–5
Black, Fischer 15
block-chain technology 125
boom and bust cycles 30, 31, 71, 86–7, 128
Bretton Woods system: asymmetric trade surpluses and 105; end of 19; enduring problems of 104–5; evolution of 12, 103–4
Broz, Lawrence 119
Brunnermeier, Markus 87
Bryan, William Jennings 10
Buiter, Willem 40, 82

Cargill, Thomas 36
cashless limits 14, 98
central bank independence (CBI) 36–7, 40, 63
central banks: criticisms of 119–20; empirical analysis of 124; establishment of 10, 35–6; evolution of 119; knowledge problem and 121–2; looking forward 128; mission creep 1; public knowledge about 1–2; public trust in 1, 2, 120–1
China 92–3
Cochrane, John 38, 67
coins 12–13, 76
commodity monies: defined 4, 7; demise of 9; inflexibility of 13; monetary policies and 14–15; price levels 18

consumer price index (CPI): asset prices included in 30–1; price indexes under inflation targeting 30; and price stability 18; property price and 30; in the USA 126, 127, *127*
convertibility 11, 15
costly state verification (CSV) 74–5
covered interest parity (CIP) 107
credit: debt financing 74–5; defined 73; equity financing 74; financial intermediaries and 73, 76; lending, historical 76; as nominal debt 74, 75
credit easing 57, 65–6
credit spreads 72
Cukierman, Alex 14
currency competition 122–4

debt: contrasted with equity for credit 74–5; costly state verification (CSV) 74–5; default risks 75; government debt 85; high inflation and public debt 37, 39–40; leverage 77–8; limited liability 78; and the tax system 75
debt deflation 72, 85–6, 88
de-linking unit of account and means of payment 67–8
Delphic forward guidance 58–9
demand shocks 28–9, 44–5, 52
demonetisation (India) 99–100
Deutsche Bundesbank 36
Diamond and Dybvig model 79, 85
digital currencies 93, 124; *see also* Bitcoin
divine coincidences 22, 29
dollar pricing 109
dollar standard system 103, 104–5
double coincidences of wants 3

Eisler, Robert 67
e-money 93
endogenous instability 71
Euler equation 21, 28, 30, 57
European Central Bank (ECB) 2, 50
Evans rule 58
exchange rate disconnect 109
exchange rate parities 104
exchange rate regimes: bilateral euro/dollar exchange rate 110–11, *111*; covered interest parity (CIP) 107; currency boards 106; dollar pricing 109; exchange rate pass-through 108–9; exogenous variations in 109–10; flexible exchange rates 108; floating regimes 106, 115–16; link with domestic interest rates 106–7; local currency pricing (LCP) 108–9; managed floats 106, 116; Optimum Currency Area theory (OCA) 114–15; pegged regimes 106, 112–13, 115–16; producer currency pricing (PCP) 108–9; as by-product of relative monetary policies 106–7; relative price adjustment 107–8; selection of 115–16; the trilemma and 107; uncovered interest parity (UIP) 106–7; valuation channels 114; *see also* external adjustments
external adjustments: of the balance of payments 111–12; in the Bretton Woods era 112; capital flows 114; and emerging markets 113; fixed exchange rates 113; floating exchange rates 113; in the Gold Standard period 112; Marshall-Lerner conditions 113; Mundell-Fleming model 112; post-Bretton Woods 112–14

Federal Reserve: criticisms of 120; establishment of 10, 84; Evans rule 58; inaction of during the Great Depression 80–1; independence of 36; interest rate corridors 42; relationship with the government 39; role of, post-financial crisis 89
Feld, Lars 95
fiat money: concept of 4–5; as financial asset 7; flexibility of 13; issue of by central banks 9–10, 11; monetary policies and 15; production of 13; and the real bills doctrine 11; *see also* paper currency
fiat money systems 19–20
financial accelerators 72, 86
financial assets 7, 114
financial cycles: boom and bust cycles 30, 31, 71, 86–7, 128; role of inside/outside money 71–2; stability and the role of central banks 72
financial intermediaries: and the global financial crisis 81; and the lender of last resort function 85; and provision of credit 73, 76; risk taking and low interest rates 88–9
financial stability: defined 72; financial cycles 71–2; inflation control by central banks 85–6; operational measures of 73; role of central banks 72; roles of inside and outside money 71–2; and wider monetary policies 87–8
fire sale externalities 79, 83
fiscal dominance: and central bank independence 40; debt defaults and 40, 87
fiscal theory of the price level: active fiscal policies 38–9; criticisms of 40; fiscal

dominance 38–9; overview of 37; passive fiscal policies 38–9; and public debt 39–40; under zero bound conditions 52–3
Fisher, Irving 86
Fisher equation 24, 30, 54
forward guidance 57, 58–9, 60–1
fractional reserve banking 80
Friedman, Milton 25–6, 43, 44, 63, 80, 108, 121, 123

Gabaix, Xavier 110
Germany 95–6
Gertler, Mark 86
Gesell, Silvio 49
Gesell tax 49–50
Gilchrist, Simon 86
global currencies 104
goal independence 36–7
gold 10, 12
Gold Standard: asymmetric behaviour and 105; and central banks 10–11; central banks' balance sheets under 11; demise of 9, 11–12, 13, 19; intrinsic problems with 12–13; monetary policies and 15; specie flow adjustments 112; as a symmetric standard 103; in the USA 126–7
government bonds: central bank purchase of under QE 60, 61, 62, 63; and the LOLR function 85
governments: debts 85; role in money creation 5
the Great Depression 80–1, 127
the Great Inflation 19, 127
the Great Moderation 18–20, 35
Greenfield-Yeager scheme 126
Gresham's Law 12–13, 122

haircuts 43
Hamilton, Alexander 92
Hayek, Friedrich 121, 122, 123, 124
hedonic improvement 32
helicopter money 63–5
hierarchies of money 9

I theory of money 87
India 99–100
inflation: annual CPI inflation in OECD countries 67; control of by central banks 22, 72, 85; and convertibility 15; CPI inflation in the USA 126, 127, *127*; and debt deflation 72, 85–6, 88; the Great Inflation 19, 127; high inflation and public debt 37, 39–40; hyper-inflation 31–2; interest rates and control of 23; low inflation and central bank independence (CBI) 37; monetary dominance assumption 19, 25, 26; movement in during financial cycles 72; output gaps 28; positive inflation targets 32–3, 50; price level determination under flexible prices 24–5, 29; relationship with money growth 14; stability of 66–7, *67*; and sticky prices 27–8; Taylor rule 15, 25, 26, 39, 51, 87, 89; very high inflation 31–2; Volcker dis-inflation 18–19, 26, 106; zero bound and inflation targets 54–5
inflation expectation creation 31, 38
inflation targeting: establishment of 19, 25–6; lack of compensation in 55; limitations of 31–2; and monetary policies 19, 25–6; and price indexes 30–1; and sticky price distortion 31
inside money 8, 9, 13, 71–2
instrument independence 36–7
interest rates: as controlled by inflation 23; corridor system 41–2, 99; and exchange rates 106–7; exchange rates and 106–7; forward guidance 57, 58–9; leaning against the wind and 88; 'low for long' (quantitative easing) 61; low interest rate implications 88–9; lower long-term rates and non-standard policies 57; negative real interest rate 48–9; paper currency and nominal negative rates 49, 94, 95; paper currency's zero interest rate 48, 49; quantitative easing (QE) 57, 60–3; real interest rate gaps 28; and risk taking 88–9; short-term interest rate controls 98–9; short-term interest rates in the world's major industrialised countries 54; time-varying interest rate on currency 49–50
international currencies 103, 104
International Monetary Fund (IMF) 103–4, 116
international monetary systems: adjustment of balance of payments imbalances 111–12; configuration of 102–3; currency competition in 123; and exchange rates 116–17; as US dollar based 104
irrelevance theorem 60, 66
Italy 76

Jackson, Andrew 120
Japan: deflationary expectations 31; second steady state 51–2; zero lower bound (ZLB) 50–1, 57

Keynes, John Maynard 104, 105
Kindleberger, Charles 6, 71

Kiyotaki, Nobuhiro 6
Kocherlakota, Narayana 6

leaning against the market 98–9
leaning against the wind 87–8
ledgers of transactions 5–6
Leeper, Eric 38
lender of last resort (LOLR) function: the Bagehot doctrine 83; central banks as 72, 82; as defence against bank runs 81; and financial intermediaries 85; and foreign debt 116; and government debt 85; historical evolution of 84; illiquidity and insolvency factors and 82; and the interbank system 84–5; penalty rates 83–4
leverage 77–8
limited liability 78
liquidity 77, 80
liquidity ratios 80
liquidity transformation 77
LM curve 21, 23–4, 98
local currency pricing (LCP) 108–9
Lucas, Robert 20, 21

macro-prudential reasons 30
Maggiori, Matteo 110
mainstream model: active and passive fiscal policy 38–9; fiscal theory 39–40; forward guidance 59; and the independence of central banks 36–7; natural rate assumption 43–6; practical implementation of 41–3; price level controls 35–41; role of collateral 42–3, 83; and supply of central bank money 41–2; unpleasant monetarist arithmetic 37–8
Marshall-Lerner conditions 113
means of exchange 3–4, 67–8
Mehrling, Perry 9
Minsky, Hyman 71
Minsky Moment 71, 87
Mishkin, Frederic 26
models, economic: mathematisation of 20; overview of 20; rational expectations concept 20–1; Real Business Cycle models 21, 27, 29; reduced form models 21; structural models 21
monetary dominance assumption 19, 25, 26
monetary economics 3
monetary policies: central bank independence (CBI) 40; commodity monies and 14–15; defined 18; Euler equation 21, 28, 30, 57; and exchange rate pass-through pricing 109; fiat money systems 15, 18; financial stability 87–8;

Fisher equation 24, 30, 54; and the Great Moderation 18–20, 35; helicopter money 63; under hysteresis 44–6; inflation targeting 19, 25–6; mainstream model 18–19, 21–2, 35; New Keynesian model 27, 29–33, 38–9; Phillips curve 22, 28, 29, 30; sticky price basic model 28–9; sticky prices 22, 26–7, 30, 31; under zero bound conditions 52–3
monetisation 39
money: characteristics of good money 6–7; circulation velocities 8, 14; coinage problems 12–13; commodity monies 4, 7, 9, 13; common currencies 115; currency competition 122–4; demand for (LM curve) 23–4, 98; elastic supply of 6; government's role in creation of 5; hierarchies of money 9; imperfect substitutability 9; as information insensitive 6–7, 9; inside money 8, 9; key functions of 3–4; ledgers of transactions 5–6; monetary value 4–5; money-less systems 3; outside money 8, 9; price levels 13–14; as substitute for ledgers of transaction 5–6; transaction costs 3; valuation of in relation to quantity 7–8, 114
money illusion 32
moneychangers 8–9
monopolistic competition 22, 29
Moore, John 6
Mundell, Robert 110–11, 115
Mundell-Fleming model 112
Mussa, Michael 110
Mussa puzzle 110

narrow banking 80
natural rate hypothesis: death of valuable firms 45; investment and 45; testing of 43–4; unemployment hysteresis 44–5
Nelson, Edward 19
network externalities 123
New Keynesian model 20, 21–2, 38–9
non-standard monetary policies: credit easing 57, 65–6; forward guidance 57, 58–9, 60–1; quantitative easing (QE) 60–3; reserve holdings 80; to solve the zero bound 57–8
numeraires 3

Odyssean forward guidance 58–9
Optimum Currency Area theory (OCA) 114–15
original sin 114
Orphanides, Athanasios 19

output gaps 28
outside money: competition between issuers of 122–4; defined 8; and hierarchies of money 9; as more than paper currency 99; price level relationship 13–14; role of in financial cycles 71–2; *see also* fiat money

paper currency: advantages of 95; counterfeiting 94; criticisms of 92; currency in circulation as a share of GDP 95–6, *96*; disadvantages of 94; endurance of 95–9; and illegal activities 94; invention of 92–3; and monetary control 97–8; nominal negative interest rates and 49, 94, 95; as outside money 99; seignorage 96–7; time-varying interest rate on currency 49–50; zero interest rates of 48, 49
Patinkin, Don 23
Phillips curve 22, 28, 29, 30
plastic money 93–4
political economy 40
portfolio balance channel 61
Posen, Adam 37, 40
price level controls 35–41
price level targeting: compensation for past misses 55–6; to counteract the zero bound 55–7; fragility of 56–7; in Sweden 56
price levels: collapse of 14; in commodity money system 18; determination of 23–4; fiscal theory of 37–8; under flexible prices 24–5; indeterminate 25; under the mainstream approach 35–6; quantity theory of money 14; relationship with outside money 13–14
producer currency pricing (PCP) 108–9
public debt: and the fiscal limit 37; and high inflation 37, 39–40

quantitative easing (QE) 57, 60–3
quantity theory of money 13–14

rational expectations concept 20–1
real bills doctrine 11
Real Business Cycle 22
Reinhart, Carmen 87
relative price adjustment 107–8
Ricardian equivalence 64
Ricardo, David 64
risk premia: credit easing 57, 65–6; and non-standard monetary policies 57

risk sharing 74
Rogoff, Ken 36, 87, 94, 100
rollover risks 85

Sannikov, Yuliy 87
Sargent, Tom 13
Schwartz, Anna 80, 123
secular international problem 105
self-correcting monetary standards 126, 128
silver standard 10
Sims, Chris 40
special drawing rights (SDR) 104
sticky prices: asset prices 30–1; defined 22; degrees of stickiness 27–8; explanations for 26; and inflation targeting 31; and monetary policies 26–7, 30; shock dependency 27, 28–9; sticky price basic model 28–9
stores of value 3–4
Summers, Larry 32–3
sunspot equilibria 79
sunspots 78
supply shocks 28–9, 52
Svensson, Lars 88
Sveriges Riksbank 10
Sweden 56

Taylor, John 89, 122
Taylor rule 15, 25, 26, 39, 51, 87, 89, 122
the Great Deviation 89
time inconsistency 36
trade shocks 108
Triffin, Robert 104–5
Triffin dilemma 104–5
trust: in central banks 1, 2, 120–1; and inside money 9; and ledgers of transaction 5
Tucker, Sir Paul 82

uncovered interest parity (UIP) 106–7
unemployment 44–5
United States of America (USA): bilateral euro/dollar exchange rate 110–11, *111*; bimetallic standard (historical) 126; CPI inflation 126, 127, *127*; exorbitant privilege of 105; Gold Standard in 126–7; monetary policy independence 104; Volcker dis-inflation 18–19, 26, 106; *see also* Federal Reserve
units of account 3–4, 67–8
unpleasant monetarist arithmetic 38
Uribe, Marin 51

Velde, Francois 13
virtual currencies *see* digital currencies
Volcker, Paul 18–19, 26

Wallace, Neil 60
Wicksell, Knut 56
Woodford, Michael 98–9
Wren-Lewis, Simon 65

zero lower bound (ZLB): circumvention policies 53; credit easing 57, 65–6; defined 48–9; de-linking unit of account and means of payment 67–8; forward guidance 57, 58–9, 60–1; helicopter money 63–5; inflation targets 54–5; Japan 50–1, 57; monetary policies under 52–3; monetary/fiscal policies balances 52–3; need for solution to 128; nominal short-term interest rate adjustments 50; non-standard monetary policies and 57–8; paper currency and negative interest rates 49, 94, 95; paradox of toil 52; perils of Taylor rules 51–2; price level targeting 55–7; quantitative easing (QE) 57, 60–3; second steady state 51–2; supply and demand shocks 52; and the Taylor rule 51; time-varying interest rate on currency 49–50

Taylor & Francis eBooks

Helping you to choose the right eBooks for your Library

Add Routledge titles to your library's digital collection today. Taylor and Francis ebooks contains over 50,000 titles in the Humanities, Social Sciences, Behavioural Sciences, Built Environment and Law.

Choose from a range of subject packages or create your own!

Benefits for you
- Free MARC records
- COUNTER-compliant usage statistics
- Flexible purchase and pricing options
- All titles DRM-free.

Benefits for your user
- Off-site, anytime access via Athens or referring URL
- Print or copy pages or chapters
- Full content search
- Bookmark, highlight and annotate text
- Access to thousands of pages of quality research at the click of a button.

REQUEST YOUR FREE INSTITUTIONAL TRIAL TODAY

Free Trials Available
We offer free trials to qualifying academic, corporate and government customers.

eCollections – Choose from over 30 subject eCollections, including:

Archaeology	Language Learning
Architecture	Law
Asian Studies	Literature
Business & Management	Media & Communication
Classical Studies	Middle East Studies
Construction	Music
Creative & Media Arts	Philosophy
Criminology & Criminal Justice	Planning
Economics	Politics
Education	Psychology & Mental Health
Energy	Religion
Engineering	Security
English Language & Linguistics	Social Work
Environment & Sustainability	Sociology
Geography	Sport
Health Studies	Theatre & Performance
History	Tourism, Hospitality & Events

For more information, pricing enquiries or to order a free trial, please contact your local sales team:
www.tandfebooks.com/page/sales

The home of Routledge books

www.tandfebooks.com